BIBLE
STUDY
made simple!

"Then you will know the truth,
and the truth will set you free."
John 8:32

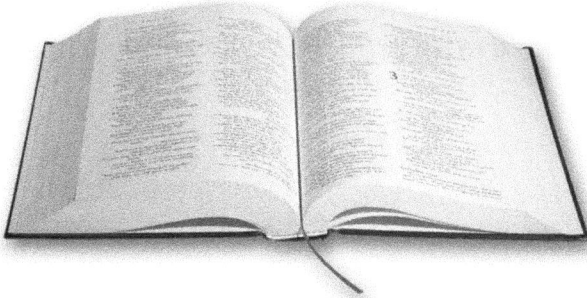

WESLEY PIERCE

Direct Author
7025 County Road 46A, Suite 1071
Lake Mary, FL 32746
www.DirectAuthor.com
877-266-5554

ISBN: 978-1-57472-500-1
Library of Congress Control Number: 2011925252

For more info or to order book copies, go to:
www.biblestudy-madesimple.com

Table of Contents

Introduction

The wisdom of God's Word speaks for itself in 24 major life-topics, each with dozens of related Scriptures grouped together into a simple, easy-to-read, concentrated format.

Gathered from various books of the Bible, the life-topics explain God's principles for the most important subjects pertaining to life and death on planet earth—*principles given only by God in the best interests of his creation.* They are able to edify and enlighten, and will establish a strong self-identity and sense of purpose for anybody who learns from them.

Readers will quickly understand the highlights of God's work throughout history to reconcile the human race back to himself, including the central focus of the Bible... the grace and peace offered to all people through the life, death, and resurrection of Jesus Christ.

It is truly sad and regretful that most people are not taught these basic truths prior to adulthood, saving millions of us from countless years or whole lifetimes mainly in pursuit of what is temporary; what will pass away.

But, young or old, now is surely a better time to start than never. So, for anyone interested in gaining an inner spirit of peace and fulfillment, let the light from these pages

shine into your heart. Everything needed to be accepted by
God, and to personally know Him is included.

Wesley Pierce,
researcher/author

"Then you will know the truth,
and the truth will set you free" –John 8:32

Bible = Word of God

Heb 1:1-3

1) In the past God spoke to our forefathers through the prophets at many times and in various ways,
2) *but in these last days he has spoken to us by his Son,* whom he appointed heir of all things, and through whom he made the universe.
3) *The Son is the radiance of God's glory and the exact representation of his being,* sustaining all things by his powerful word. After he had provided purification for sins, he sat down at the right hand of the Majesty in heaven.

2Pet 3:1-2

1) Dear friends, this is now my second letter to you. I have written both of them as reminders to stimulate you to wholesome thinking.
2) *I want you to recall the words spoken in the past by the holy prophets and the command given by our Lord and Savior through your apostles.*

   (the 12 apostles lived and traveled with Christ for about 3 years, "up close and personal". Ample opportunities to write down his words)

Luke 1:1-4

1) Many have undertaken to draw up an account of the things that have been fulfilled among us,

2) *just as they were handed down to us by those who from the first were eyewitnesses and servants of the word.*

3) *Therefore, since I myself have carefully investigated everything from the beginning, it seemed good also to me to write an orderly account for you,* most excellent Theophilus,

4) *so that you may know the certainty of the things you have been taught.*

(Luke, a doctor who sometimes traveled with Paul, assures us his account came from *eyewitnesses of Christ* and that its teachings were orderly and certain) See next entry.

2Pet 1:16-18 & 20-21

16) We did not follow cleverly invented stories when we told you about the power and coming of our Lord Jesus Christ, *but we were eyewitnesses of his majesty.*

17) For he received honor and glory from God the Father when the voice came to him from the Majestic Glory, saying, "This is my Son, whom I love; with him I am well pleased."

18) *We ourselves heard this voice that came from heaven when we were with him on the sacred mountain.*

...20) *Above all, you must understand that no prophecy of Scripture came about by the prophet's own interpretation.*

21) *For prophecy never had its origin in the will of man, but men spoke from God as they were carried along by the Holy Spirit.*

2Tim 3:16-17

16) *All Scripture is God-breathed* and is useful for teaching, rebuking, correcting and training in righteousness,

17) so that the man of God may be thoroughly equipped for every good work.

Rom 15:4

4) *For everything that was written in the past was written to teach us, so that through endurance and the encouragement of the Scriptures we might have hope.*

John 19:26-27

26) When Jesus saw his mother there, and the disciple whom he loved standing nearby, he said to his mother, "Dear woman, here is your son,"

27) and to the disciple, "Here is your mother." *From that time on, this disciple took her into his home.*

(John, the disciple above, had *direct dialogue* with Christ's mother after his crucifixion, she being the only person who knew him from birth and for all 33 years of his life on earth)

John 21:24

24) *This is the disciple who testifies to these things and who wrote them down. We know that his testimony is true.*

(also John, testifying that the writings in his book are accurate. Similar to Luke 1:1-4 above)

Gal 1:11-12

11) I want you to know, brothers, that the gospel I preached is not something that man made up.

12) *I did not receive it from any man, nor was I taught it; rather, I received it by revelation from Jesus Christ.*

(Paul, the "13th apostle" because he was chosen after Christ's death and resurrection, is the writer here)

1Ths 2:13

13) And we also thank God continually because, when you received the word of God, which you heard from us, *you accepted it not as the word of men, but as it actually is, the word of God, which is at work in you who believe.*

Isa 55:10-11

10) As the rain and the snow come down from heaven, and do not return to it without watering the earth and making it bud and flourish, so that it yields seed for the sower and bread for the eater,

11) *so is my word that goes out from my mouth: It will not return to me empty, but will accomplish what I desire and achieve the purpose for which I sent it.*

1Cor 4:6

6) Now, brothers, I have applied these things to myself and Apollos for your benefit, so that you may learn from us the meaning of the saying, *"Do not go beyond what is written."* Then you will not take pride in one man over against another.

(many voices and opinions are going forth in today's world of computers, news and entertainment media. The apostle Paul reminds us to compare what is seen, heard, and read to the Scriptures in order to discern real truth)

Heb 4:12-13

12) For the word of God is living and active. Sharper than any double-edged sword, it penetrates even to dividing soul and spirit, joints and marrow; it judges the thoughts and attitudes of the heart.

13) Nothing in all creation is hidden from God's sight. Everything is uncovered and laid bare before the eyes of him to whom we must give account.

2Tim 2:15

15) Do your best to present yourself to God as one approved, a workman who does not need to be ashamed and *who correctly handles the word of truth.*

John 8:32

32) *"Then you will know the truth, and the truth will set you free."*

John 20:30-31

30) Jesus did many other miraculous signs *in the presence of his disciples,* which are not recorded in this book.

31) *But these are written that you may believe that Jesus is the Christ, the Son of God, and that by believing you may have life in his name.*

1Cor 1:18

18) For the message of the cross is foolishness to those who are perishing, *but to us who are being saved it is the power of God.*

Col 3:16

16) Let the word of Christ dwell in you richly as you teach and admonish one another with all wisdom, and as you sing psalms, hymns and spiritual songs with gratitude in your hearts to God.

1Pet 1:24-25

24) For, "All men are like grass, and all their glory is like the flowers of the field; the grass withers and the flowers fall,

25) *but the word of the Lord stands forever."* And this is the word that was preached to you.

*Note: *italics* added to relate to topic title; author comments in parentheses to clarify

Evidence God exists

Psa 19:1-4

1) *The heavens declare the glory of God; the skies proclaim the work of his hands.*
2) Day after day they pour forth speech; night after night they display knowledge.
3) *There is no speech or language where their voice is not heard.*
4) Their voice goes out into all the earth, their words to the ends of the world. In the heavens he has pitched a tent for the sun,

Psa 8:3-4

3) *When I consider your heavens, the work of your fingers, the moon and the stars, which you have set in place,*
4) what is man that you are mindful of him, the son of man that you care for him?

Act 14:16-17

16) In the past, he let all nations go their own way.
17) *Yet he has not left himself without testimony: He has shown kindness by giving you rain from heaven and crops in their seasons*; he provides you with plenty of food and fills your hearts with joy."

Rom 1:18-21

18) The wrath of God is being revealed from heaven against all the godlessness and wickedness of men who suppress the truth by their wickedness,

19) since what may be known about God is plain to them, because God has made it plain to them.

20) *For since the creation of the world God's invisible qualities—his eternal power and divine nature—have been clearly seen, being understood from what has been made, so that men are without excuse.*

21) For although they knew God, they neither glorified him as God nor gave thanks to him, but their thinking became futile and their foolish hearts were darkened.

Eccl 11:5

5) As you do not know the path of the wind, or how the body is formed in a mother's womb, *so you cannot understand the work of God, the Maker of all things.*

Psa 139:13-14

13) For you created my inmost being; you knit me together in my mother's womb.

14) I praise you because *I am fearfully and wonderfully made*; your works are wonderful, I know that full well.

(just reflect on the inner intricacy of the human body. Then imagine yourself or anyone else attempting to create a "living, breathing" human being, not a metal-and-wires robot, *plus* all the other animals, fish, birds, and insects. Then add in outdoor nature such as trees, flowers, grass, fruits and vegetables, which also have *life* in them and are not man-made from plastic.

If Mankind is known to have the highest intelligence on earth, yet we cannot create anything with *life-giving* blood or sap flowing through it, can the thousands upon thousands of species truly have evolved from microscopic amoebas simply by chance?

Without a higher-power Creator, common sense makes the question seem foolish to even ask. The amoebas would have had to be smarter than humans to end up as all the "alive" species on earth which do contain *life-giving* blood or sap in them. And if they are smarter, *from where did amoebas originate*? Quite a guessing game, or perhaps imagination) see entries below.

Psa 104:24

24) How many are your works, O LORD! In wisdom you made them all; the earth is full of your creatures.

Col 1:16

16) For by him all things were created: things in heaven and on earth, visible and invisible, whether thrones or powers or rulers or authorities; all things were created by him and for him.

Heb 11:6

6) And without faith it is impossible to please God, because *anyone who comes to him must believe that he exists and that he rewards those who earnestly seek him.*

Job 38:1-11

1) Then the LORD answered Job out of the storm. He said:
2) *"Who is this that darkens my counsel with words without knowledge?*
3) *Brace yourself like a man; I will question you, and you shall answer me.*

4) "Where were you when I laid the earth's foundation? Tell me, if you understand.
5) Who marked off its dimensions? Surely you know! Who stretched a measuring line across it?
6) On what were its footings set, or who laid its cornerstone—

7) while the morning stars sang together and all the angels shouted for joy?

8) "Who shut up the sea behind doors when it burst forth from the womb,

9) when I made the clouds its garment and wrapped it in thick darkness,

10) when I fixed limits for it and set its doors and bars in place,

11) when I said, 'This far you may come and no farther; here is where your proud waves halt'?

Job 38:18-41

18) Have you comprehended the vast expanses of the earth? *Tell me, if you know all this.*

19) "What is the way to the abode of light? And where does darkness reside?

20) Can you take them to their places? Do you know the paths to their dwellings?

21) *Surely you know, for you were already born! You have lived so many years!*

22) "Have you entered the storehouses of the snow or seen the storehouses of the hail,

23) which I reserve for times of trouble, for days of war and battle?

24) What is the way to the place where the lightning is dispersed, or the place where the east winds are scattered over the earth?

25) Who cuts a channel for the torrents of rain, and a path for the thunderstorm,

26) to water a land where no man lives, a desert with no one in it,

27) to satisfy a desolate wasteland and make it sprout with grass?

28) Does the rain have a father? Who fathers the drops of dew?

29) From whose womb comes the ice? Who gives birth to the frost from the heavens

30) when the waters become hard as stone, when the surface of the deep is frozen?

31) "Can you bind the beautiful Pleiades? Can you loose the cords of Orion?

32) Can you bring forth the constellations in their seasons or lead out the Bear with its cubs?

33) Do you know the laws of the heavens? Can you set up God's dominion over the earth?

34) "Can you raise your voice to the clouds and cover yourself with a flood of water?

35) Do you send the lightning bolts on their way? Do they report to you, 'Here we are'?

36) Who endowed the heart with wisdom or gave understanding to the mind?

37) Who has the wisdom to count the clouds? Who can tip over the water jars of the heavens

38) when the dust becomes hard and the clods of earth stick together?

39) "Do you hunt the prey for the lioness and satisfy the hunger of the lions

40) when they crouch in their dens or lie in wait in a thicket?

41) Who provides food for the raven when its young cry out to God and wander about for lack of food?

(it is abundantly clear... "The fear of the Lord is the beginning of knowledge"—Prov 1:7)

*Note: *Italics* added to relate to topic title; author comments in parentheses to clarify

Satan - darkness and death

Ezek 28:12-17

12) "Son of man, take up a lament concerning the king of Tyre and say to him: 'This is what the Sovereign LORD says: "'You were the model of perfection, full of wisdom and perfect in beauty.

13) You were in Eden, the garden of God; every precious stone adorned you: ruby, topaz and emerald, chrysolite, onyx and jasper, sapphire, turquoise and beryl. Your settings and mountings were made of gold; on the day you were created they were prepared.

14) You were anointed as a guardian cherub, for so I ordained you. You were on the holy mount of God; you walked among the fiery stones.

15) *You were blameless in your ways from the day you were created till wickedness was found in you.*

16) Through your widespread trade you were filled with violence, and you sinned. *So I drove you in disgrace from the mount of God, and I expelled you,* O guardian cherub, from among the fiery stones.

17) Your heart became proud on account of your beauty, and you corrupted your wisdom because of your splendor. *So I threw you to the earth*; I made a spectacle of you before kings.

(most Bible students regard these verses in Ezekiel and the next entry in Isaiah to be symbolic descriptions of God expelling the former morning star, Satan, from heaven down to earth as his new place of habitation... see Job 1: 6-7 below. He could no longer remain in God's presence due to his ego and pride to be "The Boss", #1 in the universe above God.)

Isa 14:12-14

12) How you have fallen from heaven, O morning star, son of the dawn! *You have been cast down to the earth*, you who once laid low the nations!

13) You said in your heart, "I will ascend to heaven; *I will raise my throne above the stars of God*; I will sit enthroned on the mount of assembly, on the utmost heights of the sacred mountain.

14) I will ascend above the tops of the clouds; *I will make myself like the Most High*."

(see comment above about Satan's ego and pride...remembering Mankind will also be expelled from God's presence unless we accept his offer to live again through the sacrifice of Jesus Christ, <u>our substitute</u> in receiving punishment for sins—necessary in God's eyes because of our own ego and pride to be "The Boss".

How do we do that? By ignoring or disobeying the Scriptures, which are the Creator's guidelines for Mankind in our *daily* lifestyles, habits, and inner attitudes. Hundreds of millions of people everywhere rarely or never open the Bible to understand the message of salvation, or what our "owner's manual" states about human behavior)

Luke 10:18

18) He replied, "I saw Satan fall like lightning from heaven."

Job 1:6-7

6) One day the angels came to present themselves before the LORD, and Satan also came with them.

7) The LORD said to Satan, "Where have you come from?" *Satan answered the LORD, "From roaming through the earth and going back and forth in it."*

(although we cannot see spiritual beings, the Scriptures clearly state they do exist)

Eph 6:12

12) For our struggle is not against flesh and blood, but against the rulers, against the authorities, *against the powers of this dark world and against the spiritual forces of evil in the heavenly realms.*

2Cor 4:4

4) *The god of this age has blinded the minds of unbelievers,* so that they cannot see the light of the gospel of the glory of Christ, *who is the image of God.*

("blinded minds" because we yield to Satan's temptations, which come through the ungodly customs and habits of society around us; a "follow-the-herd" mentality. The end result is stated in the entry below, but the *solution* is shown in the second entry below)

Rom 5:12

12) Therefore, just as sin entered the world through one man, and death through sin, and in this way death came to all men, because all sinned—

2Cor 6:17-18

17) *"Therefore come out from them and be separate, says the Lord. Touch no unclean thing, and I will receive you."*

18) *"I will be a Father to you, and you will be my sons and daughters, says the Lord Almighty."*

Luke 4:5-8

5) The devil led him up to a high place and showed him in an instant all the kingdoms of the world.
6) And he said to him, *"I will give you all their authority and splendor, for it has been given to me, and I can give it to anyone I want to.*
7) So if you worship me, it will all be yours."
8) Jesus answered, *"It is written: 'Worship the Lord your God and serve him only.'"*

(we can all learn a lesson from Christ by noting he answered the temptation with the Scriptures..."it is written", our guiding light in a world full of human opinions)

Act 26:16-18

16) "Now get up and stand on your feet. I have appeared to you to appoint you as a servant and as a witness of what you have seen of me and what I will show you.
17) I will rescue you from your own people and from the Gentiles. I am sending you to them
18) *to open their eyes and turn them from darkness to light, and from the power of Satan to God, so that they may receive forgiveness of sins and a place among those who are sanctified by faith in me.'*

(through Paul and other messengers throughout history, God has offered salvation to the rest of the world, not just Israel)

John 12:31

31) Now is the time for judgment on this world; *now the prince of this world will be driven out.*

(Jesus, referring to his eminent crucifixion and resurrection, which would *defeat death and Satan*)

Heb 2:14

14) Since the children have flesh and blood, he too shared in their humanity *so that by his death he might destroy him who holds the power of death— that is, the devil—*

1John 3:7-8

7) Dear children, do not let anyone lead you astray. He who does what is right is righteous, just as he is righteous.

8) He who does what is sinful is of the devil, because the devil has been sinning from the beginning. *The reason the Son of God appeared was to destroy the devil's work.*

1Pet 5:8-9

8) Be self-controlled and alert. *Your enemy the devil prowls around like a roaring lion looking for someone to devour.*

9) Resist him, standing firm in the faith, because you know that *your brothers throughout the world are undergoing the same kind of sufferings.*

Jam 4:7

7) Submit yourselves, then, to God. *Resist the devil, and he will flee from you.*

*Note: *italics* added to relate to topic title; author comments in parentheses to clarify

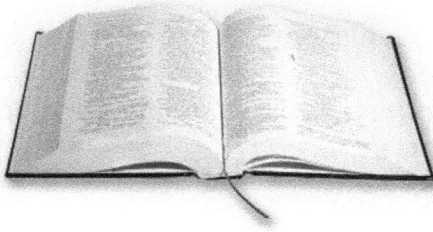

Innocence lost - fall of Mankind

Gen 1:1

1) In the beginning God created the heavens and the earth.

Gen 1:26-27

26) Then God said, "Let us make man in our image, in our likeness, and let them rule over the fish of the sea and the birds of the air, over the livestock, over all the earth, and over all the creatures that move along the ground."

27) So God created man in his own image, in the image of God he created him; male and female he created them.

Gen 2:7

7) the LORD God formed the man from the dust of the ground and *breathed into his nostrils the breath of life,* and the man became a living being.

Gen 2:15-17

15) The LORD God took the man and put him in the Garden of Eden to work it and take care of it.

16) And the LORD God commanded the man, *"You are free to eat from any tree in the garden;*

17) *but you must not eat from the tree of the knowledge of good and evil, for when you eat of it you will surely die."*

("free to eat from any tree in the garden" included the tree of life; originally they would not have died physically had they obeyed God)

Gen 2:22-25

22) Then the LORD God made a woman from the rib he had taken out of the man, and he brought her to the man.

23) The man said, "This is now bone of my bones and flesh of my flesh; she shall be called 'woman,' for she was taken out of man."

24) For this reason a man will leave his father and mother and be united to his wife, and they will become one flesh.

25) *The man and his wife were both naked, and they felt no shame.*

(They were innocent and pure when first created)

Gen 3:1-5

1) Now the serpent was more crafty than any of the wild animals the LORD God had made. He said to the woman, "Did God really say, 'You must not eat from any tree in the garden'?"

2) The woman said to the serpent, "We may eat fruit from the trees in the garden,

3) but God did say, 'You must not eat fruit from the tree that is in the middle of the garden, and you must not touch it, or you will die.'"

4) "You will not surely die," the serpent said to the woman.

5) "For God knows that when you eat of it your eyes will be opened, *and you will be like God, knowing good and evil.*"

(since there were no other human beings on earth, the unseen spirit of Satan spoke through the serpent, which Eve could see, with an appeal to ego/pride—their downfall)

Gen 3:6-8

6) When the woman saw that the fruit of the tree was good for food and pleasing to the eye, and also desirable for gaining wisdom, she took some and ate it. She also gave some to her husband, who was with her, and he ate it.

7) *Then the eyes of both of them were opened, and they realized they were naked*; so they sewed fig leaves together and made coverings for themselves.

8) *.....and they hid from the LORD God* among the trees of the garden.

   (they failed the test of obedience God had allowed through Satan's temptation. God's spirit of innocence then left them, replaced instead by Satan's spirit of shame and fear when "their eyes were opened, and they hid from the LORD". Thus, the first-ever sin, or disobedience of God.

   As a result their relationship with the Lord was separated; they became dead to God's inner spirit, and their physical bodies would also eventually die. Worst of all, their self-centered "infection" by Satan's spirit would be passed on to all human offspring, as each generation to come would find its own ways of disobeying God)

Gen 3:13-19

13) Then the LORD God said to the woman, "What is this you have done?" The woman said, "The serpent deceived me, and I ate."

14) So the LORD God said to the serpent, "Because you have done this, *"Cursed are you above all the livestock and all the wild animals! You will crawl on your belly and you will eat dust all the days of your life.*

15) And I will put enmity between you and the woman, and between your offspring and hers; he will crush your head, and you will strike his heel."

16) To the woman he said, *"I will greatly increase your pains in childbearing; with pain you will give birth to children. Your desire will be for your husband, and he will rule over you."*

17) To Adam he said, "Because you listened to your wife and ate from the tree about which I commanded you, 'You must not eat of it,' *"Cursed is the ground because of you; through painful toil you will eat of it all the days of your life.*

18) *It will produce thorns and thistles for you, and you will eat the plants of the field.*

19) *By the sweat of your brow you will eat your food until you return to the ground, since from it you were taken; for dust you are and to dust you will return."*

(it is obvious God regards our disobedience of Him *more seriously* than we human beings do...the consequences were enormous for every single person who would follow.

Death, weeds, difficulty supplying enough food, storms/ bad weather, hail, drought, and disasters such as hurricanes, tornadoes, earthquakes, floods, etc. can all likely be attributed to the random forces of nature God set into motion as a result, not only of Adam and Eve's curse, but Mankind's continuing errant ways ever since that first failure to obey) see entries below.

Gen 3:22-24

22) And the LORD God said, "The man has now become like one of us, knowing good and evil. *He must not be allowed to reach out his hand and take also from the tree of life and eat, and live forever."*

23) *So the LORD God banished him from the Garden of Eden to work the ground from which he had been taken.*

24) After he drove the man out, he placed on the east
    side of the Garden of Eden cherubim and a flaming
    sword flashing back and forth *to guard the way to
    the tree of life.*

(innocence had been lost; death would now reign over
mankind...they no longer had access to the tree of life. The
process of physical aging and death began instead, starting
with the first generations of people living more than 900
years, then gradually winding down through time as they
became more and more corrupted in God's eyes)

Gen 6:1-3

1) When men began to increase in number on the earth
   and daughters were born to them,
2) the sons of God saw that the daughters of men were
   beautiful, *and they married any of them they chose.*
3) Then the LORD said, "My Spirit will not contend
   with man forever, for he is mortal; his days will be a
   hundred and twenty years."

(God warns us about being unequally yoked...see 2Cor
6:14-15. The "sons of God" most likely refers to Believers
in God descended from Seth, Adam and Eve's godly son
born after Abel was murdered, while the "daughters of
men" are most likely the non-believers descended from
ungodly Cain, who killed Abel...see Gen 4:25-26)

Gen 6:5-9

5) *The LORD saw how great man's wickedness on the
   earth had become,* and that every inclination of the
   thoughts of his heart was only evil all the time.
6) *The LORD was grieved that he had made man on
   the earth, and his heart was filled with pain.*
7) So the LORD said, "I will wipe mankind, whom I
   have created, from the face of the earth—men and
   animals, and creatures that move along the ground,
   and birds of the air—for I am grieved that I have
   made them."

8) *But Noah found favor in the eyes of the LORD.*

9) This is the account of Noah. Noah was a righteous man, blameless among the people of his time, *and he walked with God.*

Gen 6:11-14

11) Now the earth was corrupt in God's sight and was full of violence.

12) God saw how corrupt the earth had become, *for all the people on earth had corrupted their ways.*

13) So God said to Noah, "I am going to put an end to all people, for the earth is filled with violence because of them. I am surely going to destroy both them and the earth.

14) So make for yourself an ark of cypress wood; make rooms in it and coat it with pitch inside and out."

Gen 6:22

22) Noah did everything just as God commanded him.

Gen 7:1

1) The LORD then said to Noah, "Go into the ark, you and your whole family, *because I have found you righteous in this generation.*

Gen 7:11-12

11) In the six hundredth year of Noah's life, on the seventeenth day of the second month—on that day *all the springs of the great deep burst forth, and the floodgates of the heavens were opened.*

12) *And rain fell on the earth forty days and forty nights.*

(water not only came down from the skies, but from be-low-ground springs as well)

Gen 7:21-23

21) *Every living thing that moved on the earth perished—* birds, livestock, wild animals, all the creatures that swarm over the earth, and all mankind.

22) Everything on dry land that had the breath of life in its nostrils died.

23) *Every living thing on the face of the earth was wiped out*; men and animals and the creatures that move along the ground and the birds of the air were wiped from the earth. *Only Noah was left, and those with him in the ark.*

(this total corruption of the human race took approximately 1600 years from the time of Adam's creation to Noah's flood. The re-start after the flood would last only about 400 more years before Mankind once again became fully corrupted and spiritually dead.

This caused God to make a *third attempt,* following Adam and Noah, at gaining people's allegiance by calling Abraham and the Israelites to become God's "chosen people"...see Exo 19:5-6. That in turn would go back and forth from blessings to failure dozens of times over the next 2000 years during the Old Testament age, depending often on whether the nation's reigning king was godly or corrupt, with the citizens usually following his example.

God finally lost patience with the Israelites as well, because in the end their religious leaders—priests, pharisees, sanhedrin—became as ungodly as the bad kings had been, and were especially scolded by Jesus Christ himself, which gave them one of many reasons to crucify him. After Christ's resurrection from the dead, the nation was forsaken by God when he allowed the Romans to conquer the land and destroy the temple in 70 A.D.

Mankind then entered what will likely be *the final phase* of God's attempts to redeem the human race unto himself, sending forth the message of reconciliation through Christ to the rest of the world, starting with the original

12 Apostles and Paul, on down through other messengers as more countries became populated.

Now another 2000+ years have passed since the Lord came to this earth. One has to wonder how much longer God will continue waiting with this last dispensation of his grace known as the "times of the Gentiles"...see Eph 3:6.

The message of salvation in Christ has gone, or is now going, to every nation on earth. One day all bases will be covered; then it is probable God will no longer have a reason to keep on waiting, especially in view of the ever-increasing ungodliness displayed by people everywhere.

But how long before God puts an end to it, as in the days of Noah? Before his last bit of patience finally runs out? Nobody knows...see Mat 24:36. However, we can simply observe what is taking place with the current human race all over the world, *as compared to what the Scriptures state our behavior should be like*, then use common sense to judge whether it is more likely to be sooner—years/decades, or later—centuries)

2Pet 3:9

9) The Lord is not slow in keeping his promise, as some understand slowness. *He is* patient with you, not wanting anyone to perish, but everyone to come to repentance.

(a message to all people for our own well-being—get serious, sober up, be prepared. The final destruction of planet earth will be by blazing fire, not cool water as in Noah's Time; see 2Pet 3:3-12. We can be sure...it will not be pleasant for those who miss the call to be with God in the next life)

*Note: *italics* added to relate to topic title; author comments in parentheses to clarify

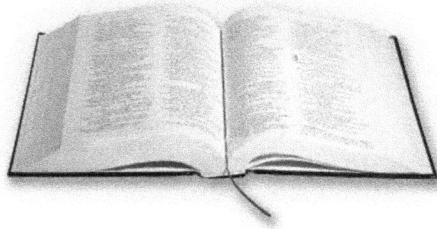

Why God is invisible

Job 23:8-9

8) "But if I go to the east, he is not there; if I go to the west, I do not find him.

9) When he is at work in the north, I do not see him; when he turns to the south, I catch no glimpse of him.

1Tim 6:15-16

15) ...God, the blessed and only Ruler, the King of kings and Lord of lords,

16) who alone is immortal and *who lives in unapproachable light, whom no one has seen or can see.* To him be honor and might forever. Amen.

(think of staring at light much brighter than the sun... we would all become blind, or perhaps incinerated if we were too close)

Exo 33:18-20

18) Then Moses said, "Now show me your glory."

19) And the LORD said, "I will cause all my goodness to pass in front of you, and I will proclaim my name, the LORD, in your presence. I will have mercy on whom I will have mercy, and I will have compassion on whom I will have compassion.

20) But," he said, *"you cannot see my face, for no one may see me and live."* (see next entry)

Exo 19:20-21

20) The LORD descended to the top of Mount Sinai and called Moses to the top of the mountain. So Moses went up

21) and the LORD said to him, *"Go down and warn the people so they do not force their way through to see the LORD and many of them perish.*

(shows the seriousness with which God regards our wrongdoings and rebellious ways. He will not allow people who ignore or disobey him into his presence, even though he is more willing to forgive our shortcomings than to punish us.

Only his representative, Moses, was exempt from immediate death; however, in that age around 1500 B.C. Moses also had to be forgiven regularly through animal sacrifices after coming down from the mountain, along with the rest of the Israelites. Today, forgiveness is through Christ's sacrifice, not animals...see 1John 4: 9-10)

Ezra 9:15

15) O LORD, God of Israel, you are righteous! We are left this day as a remnant. Here we are before you in our guilt, *though because of it not one of us can stand in your presence."*

John 1:18

18) No one has ever seen God, but God the One and Only, who is at the Father's side, *has made him known.* (see next entry)

John 12:44-45

44) Then Jesus cried out, "When a man believes in me, he does not believe in me only, but in the one who sent me.

45) *When he looks at me, he sees the one who sent me."*

(his physical body was human, but conceived by God's Spirit. However; his wisdom, thoughts and attitudes, self-control, and obedience came from that same Spirit working inside him, for he was given *"the Spirit without limit"*...see John 3:34. So, we can say God actually did become physically visible during the approximate 33 years of Christ's human life on earth)

Col 1:15-16

15) *He is the image of the invisible God,* the firstborn over all creation.
16) For by him all things were created: things in heaven and on earth, *visible and invisible,* whether thrones or powers or rulers or authorities; all things were created by him and for him.

John 4:24

24) God is spirit, and his worshipers must worship in spirit and in truth."

Heb 11:3

3) By faith we understand that the universe was formed at God's command, so that *what is seen was not made out of what was visible.*

Heb 11:6

6) And without faith it is impossible to please God, because anyone who comes to him must believe that he exists and that *he rewards those who earnestly seek him.*

*Note: *italics* added to relate to topic title; author comments in parentheses to clarify

All people fall short of God's expectations

Mark 7:20-23

20) He went on: *"What comes out of a man is what makes him 'unclean.'*

21) For from within, out of men's hearts, come evil thoughts, sexual immorality, theft, murder, adultery,

22) greed, malice, deceit, lewdness, envy, slander, arrogance and folly.

23) *All these evils come from inside and make a man "unclean."'*

(to enlighten ourselves, look up all words listed above in a dictionary and learn it does not take a *major* offense to defile us in God's eyes, although some are major. Nevertheless, Christ took our punishment for us on the cross so his righteousness would wash away our "uncleanness")

John 2:23-25

23) Now while he was in Jerusalem at the Passover Feast, many people saw the miraculous signs he was doing and believed in his name.

24) *But Jesus would not entrust himself to them, for he knew all men.*

25) *He did not need man's testimony about man, for he knew what was in a man.*

Rom 5:12

12) Therefore, just as sin entered the world through one man, and death through sin, *and in this way death came to all men, because all sinned—*

Eccl 7:20

20) There is not a righteous man on earth who does what is right and never sins.

Eccl 7:29

29) This only have I found: God made mankind upright, *but men have gone in search of many schemes."* (see entry below)

Isa 65:2

2) *All day long* I have held out my hands to an obstinate people, who walk in ways not good, *pursuing their own imaginations—*

(e.g., do-my-own-thing...no boundaries allowed...I and me are in charge...not a moment's thought acknowledging God's presence all day long, as stated)

Rom 3:23

23) for all have sinned and fall short of the glory of God,

Rom 3:14-18

14) "Their mouths are full of cursing and bitterness."
15) "Their feet are swift to shed blood;
16) ruin and misery mark their ways,
17) and the way of peace they do not know."
18) *"There is no fear of God before their eyes."*

(fear of God = respect, honor, willingness to submit to a Higher Power)

Jer 17:9-10

9) *The heart is deceitful above all things and beyond cure.* Who can understand it?

10) "I the LORD search the heart and examine the mind, to reward a man according to his conduct, according to what his deeds deserve."

Isa 29:13
13) The Lord says: "These people come near to me with their mouth and honor me with their lips, but their hearts are far from me. *Their worship of me is made up only of rules taught by men.*"

(it is imperative that a higher standard than human-level rules and opinions be honored in this world, because there are millions of people with millions of opinions. How can we know which ones are absolutely correct?

There is only one place to find the rules and opinions of almighty God, our Creator and our Superior, whose principles and judgments we can completely trust. For true wisdom and inner peace, get to know the Bible, starting with the New Testament.)

Jam 1:13-15
13) When tempted, no one should say, "God is tempting me." For God cannot be tempted by evil, nor does he tempt anyone;
14) *but each one is tempted when, by his own evil desire, he is dragged away and enticed.*
15) Then, after desire has conceived, it gives birth to sin; and sin, when it is full-grown, gives birth to death.

Luke 5:31-32
31) Jesus answered them, "It is not the healthy who need a doctor, but the sick.
32) *I have not come to call the righteous, but sinners to repentance.*"

Eph 2:1-5
1) *As for you, you were dead in your transgressions and sins,*

2) *in which you used to live when you followed the ways of this world* and of the ruler of the kingdom of the air, the spirit who is now at work in those who are disobedient.

3) *All of us also lived among them at one time, gratifying the cravings of our sinful nature and following its desires and thoughts. Like the rest, we were by nature objects of wrath.*

4) But because of his great love for us, God, who is rich in mercy,

5) made us alive with Christ *even when we were dead in transgressions*—it is by grace you have been saved.

Eph 4:17-19

17) So I tell you this, and insist on it in the Lord, that you must no longer live as the Gentiles do, in the futility of their thinking.

18) They are darkened in their understanding and separated from the life of God because of the ignorance that is in them due to the hardening of their hearts.

19) *Having lost all sensitivity, they have given themselves over to sensuality so as to indulge in every kind of impurity, with a continual lust for more.*

(a few current examples: rampant sexuality—married, unmarried, or otherwise, and *featured* everywhere through various media; over-indulgent cravings for food, drugs, alcohol, material possessions, and social status; physical appearance obsessions; celebrity "stars" as human idols.

An explosion of choices from entertainment, sports, television, computers, and cell phones which rob much of our attention and priorities necessary for a balanced mindset. Some of it is needed, but most of us go overboard with very little self- control)

1John 1:8-9

8) If we claim to be without sin, we deceive ourselves and the truth is not in us.

9) *If we confess our sins, he is faithful and just and will forgive us our sins and purify us from all unrighteousness.*

(this is the great equalizer for Mankind through God's gift of Christ as Savior who, <u>as our substitute</u>, took the punishment we each deserve in God's eyes. Since our wrongdoings and misguided attitudes multiply over an entire lifetime, we are the ones who should be crucified if He were a judge only, without forgiveness and mercy) see Psa 103:10-18 and entry below.

Lam 3:22-23

22) Because of the LORD's great love *we are not consumed, for his compassions never fail.*

23) *They are new every morning; great is your faithfulness.*

*Note: *italics* added to relate to topic title; author comments in parentheses to clarify

Blood = atonement and pardon

Exo 12:3 & 5-7 & 12-13

3) Tell the whole community of Israel that on the tenth day of this month each man is to take a lamb for his family, one for each household.

...5) The animals you choose must be year-old *males without defect*, and you may take them from the sheep or the goats.

6) Take care of them until the fourteenth day of the month, when all the people of the community of Israel must slaughter them at twilight.

7) Then they are to *take some of the blood and put it on the sides and tops of the doorframes of the houses where they eat the lambs.*

...12) "On that same night I will pass through Egypt and strike down every firstborn—both men and animals— and I will bring judgment on all the gods of Egypt. I am the LORD.

13) *The blood will be a sign for you on the houses where you are; and when I see the blood, I will pass over you.* No destructive plague will touch you when I strike Egypt.

(this first Passover, instituted by God for his chosen people at that time, the Israelites, is a preview of the role Jesus Christ would assume 1500 years later as the "lamb of God" shedding his own blood on behalf of all Mankind's salvation, putting an end to animal sacrifices permanently. Today, Christ's blood is our "sign on the doorframe" for God to passover anyone who believes in him on the day of judgment)

Lev 17:11

11) *For the life of a creature is in the blood, and I have given it to you to make atonement for yourselves on the altar; it is the blood that makes atonement for one's life.*

Heb 9:22

22) In fact, the law requires that nearly everything be cleansed with blood, *and without the shedding of blood there is no forgiveness.*

Exo 30:10

10) Once a year Aaron shall make atonement on its horns. *This annual atonement must be made with the blood of the atoning sin offering for the generations to come. It is most holy to the LORD."*

(the rule of forgiveness by animal sacrifice for Israel, prior to the crucifixion of Christ)

Gal 1:3-4

3) Grace and peace to you from God our Father and the Lord Jesus Christ,

4) *who gave himself for our sins to rescue us from the present evil age,* according to the will of our God and Father,

(the rule of forgiveness after Christ's resurrection, which was proof of another life)

Luke 22:19-20

19) And he took bread, gave thanks and broke it, and gave it to them, saying, *"This is my body given for you; do this in remembrance of me."*

20) In the same way, after the supper he took the cup, saying, *"This cup is the new covenant in my blood, which is poured out for you.*

Rom 5:8-10

8) *But God demonstrates his own love for us in this: While we were still sinners, Christ died for us.*
9) Since we have now been *justified by his blood*, how much more shall we be saved from God's wrath through him!
10) For if, when we were God's enemies, we were reconciled to him through the death of his Son, how much more, having been reconciled, shall we be saved through his life!

Col 1:19-22

19) For God was pleased to have all his fullness dwell in him,
20) and through him to reconcile to himself all things, whether things on earth or things in heaven, *by making peace through his blood, shed on the cross.*
21) Once you were alienated from God and were enemies in your minds because of your evil behavior.
22) *But now he has reconciled you by Christ's physical body through death to present you holy in his sight, without blemish and free from accusation—*

(think and re-think this truth...we can be "reconciled to God and free from accusation" through Christ's sacrifice, in spite of a lifetime of wrongdoings or ignoring him)

1John 1:7-9

7) But if we walk in the light, as he is in the light, we have fellowship with one another, *and the blood of Jesus, his Son, purifies us from all sin.*
8) If we claim to be without sin, we deceive ourselves and the truth is not in us.
9) *If we confess our sins, he is faithful and just and*

will forgive us our sins and purify us from all unrighteousness.

1Pet 1:17-21

17) Since you call on a Father who judges each man's work impartially, live your lives as strangers here in reverent fear.
18) For you know that it was not with perishable things such as silver or gold that you were redeemed from *the empty way of life handed down to you from your forefathers,*
19) *but with the precious blood of Christ, a lamb without blemish or defect.*
20) He was chosen before the creation of the world, but was revealed in these last times for your sake.
21) Through him you believe in God, who raised him from the dead and glorified him, and so your faith and hope are in God.

Heb 9:14-15

14) How much more, then, *will the blood of Christ,* who through the eternal Spirit offered himself unblemished to God, cleanse our consciences from acts that lead to death, so that we may serve the living God!
15) For this reason Christ is the mediator of a new covenant, that those who are called may receive the promised eternal inheritance—*now that he has died as a ransom to set them free* from the sins committed under the first covenant.

Rev 5:9-10

9) And they sang a new song: "You are worthy to take the scroll and to open its seals, because you were slain, *and with your blood you purchased men for God from every tribe and language and people and nation.*
10) You have made them to be a kingdom and priests to serve our God, *and they will reign on the earth.*"

(the new earth, that is, to be created after this current troubled world is destroyed and replaced at the end-of-the-age) see Rev 21:1-5.

*Note: *italics* added to relate to topic title; author comments in parentheses to clarify

Jesus Christ -
God in human form

John 1:1-2
1) In the beginning was the Word, and the Word was with God, and the Word was God.
2) He was with God in the beginning.

John 1:14
14) *The Word became flesh and made his dwelling among us.* We have seen his glory, the glory of the One and Only, who came from the Father, full of grace and truth.

Luke 1:30-35
30) But the angel said to her, "Do not be afraid, Mary, you have found favor with God.
31) You will be with child and give birth to a son, and you are to give him the name Jesus.
32) He will be great and will be called the Son of the Most High. The Lord God will give him the throne of his father David,
33) and he will reign over the house of Jacob forever; his kingdom will never end."
34) "How will this be," Mary asked the angel, "since I am a virgin?"

35) The angel answered, *"The Holy Spirit will come upon you, and the power of the Most High will overshadow you. So the holy one to be born will be called the Son of God.*

(no other person has ever been born without having a human father)

Luke 2:30-33

30) For my eyes have seen your salvation,
31) which you have prepared in the sight of all people,
32) a light for revelation to the Gentiles and for glory to your people Israel."
33) *The child's father and mother marveled at what was said about him.*

(shortly after his birth; God the Father had already prepared knowledge of a Savior)

Luke 2:40

40) And the child grew and became strong; *he was filled with wisdom, and the grace of God was upon him.*

(see John 3:34 below; Jesus received "the Spirit without limit")

Luke 2:46-47

46) After three days they found him in the temple courts, sitting among the teachers, listening to them and asking them questions.
47) *Everyone who heard him was amazed at his understanding and his answers.*

(at age 12, already filled with wisdom from God's Spirit)

1John 1:1-2

1) That which was from the beginning, *which we have heard, which we have seen with our eyes, which we have looked at and our hands have touched*—this we proclaim concerning the Word of life.

2) The life appeared; *we have seen it and testify to it, and we proclaim to you the eternal life, which was with the Father and has appeared to us.*

(Eyewitnesses, in person. The original 12 apostles observed and lived with Christ for about 3 years)

John 1:18

18) No one has ever seen God, but God the One and Only, who is at the Father's side, *has made him known.*

Col 2:8-9

8) See to it that no one takes you captive through hollow and deceptive philosophy, which depends on human tradition and the basic principles of this world rather than on Christ.

9) *For in Christ all the fullness of the Deity lives in bodily form,*

(God's Spirit, wisdom, self-control, and obedience inside a human body...the invisible God did become visible for approximately 33 years while Christ was on earth)

Heb 1:3

3) The Son is the *radiance of God's glory and the exact representation of his being,* sustaining all things by his powerful word. After he had provided purification for sins, he sat down at the right hand of the Majesty in heaven.

John 10:30

30) I and the Father are one."

John 14:6-7

6) Jesus answered, "I am the way and the truth and the life. No one comes to the Father except through me.

7) If you really knew me, you would know my Father as well. *From now on, you do know him and have seen him.*"

John 12:44-45

44) Then Jesus cried out, "When a man believes in me, he does not believe in me only, but in the one who sent me.

45) *When he looks at me, he sees the one who sent me.*

John 3:34-35

34) *For the one whom God has sent speaks the words of God, for God gives the Spirit without limit.*

35) The Father loves the Son and has placed everything in his hands.

John 12:49-50

49) For I did not speak of my own accord, *but the Father who sent me commanded me what to say and how to say it.*

50) I know that his command leads to eternal life. *So whatever I say is just what the Father has told me to say.*"

Heb 2:14-15

14) *Since the children have flesh and blood, he too shared in their humanity* so that by his death he might destroy him who holds the power of death—that is, the devil—

15) and free those who all their lives were held in slavery by their fear of death.

Rom 1:3-4

3) regarding his Son, who as to his human nature was a descendant of David,

4) and who through the Spirit of holiness *was declared with power to be the Son of God by his resurrection from the dead*: Jesus Christ our Lord.

(after his crucifixion, he was seen alive again over a 40-day period by the remaining Apostles and many others as eyewitnesses. see Acts 1:3)

John 10:37-38

37) Do not believe me unless I do what my Father does.

38) But if I do it, even though you do not believe me, *believe the miracles, that you may know and understand that the Father is in me, and I in the Father.*"

Col 1:18-20

18) And he is the head of the body, the church; he is the beginning and *the firstborn from among the dead,* so that in everything he might have the supremacy.

19) *For God was pleased to have all his fullness dwell in him,*

20) and through him to reconcile to himself all things, whether things on earth or things in heaven, by making peace through his blood, shed on the cross.

John 8:23-24

23) But he continued, *"You are from below; I am from above. You are of this world; I am not of this world.*

24) I told you that you would die in your sins; if you do not believe that I am the one I claim to be, you will indeed die in your sins."

John 16:27-28

27) No, the Father himself loves you because you have loved me and have believed that I came from God.

28) *I came from the Father and entered the world; now I am leaving the world and going back to the Father.*

*Note: *italics* added to relate to topic title; author comments in parentheses to clarify

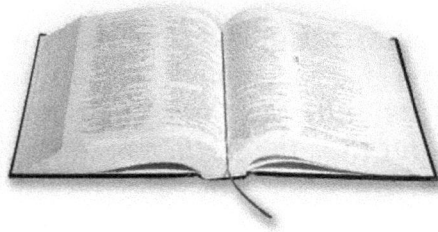

Jesus Christ - Savior for all people

Isa 53:2-12

2) He grew up before him like a tender shoot, and like a root out of dry ground. He had no beauty or majesty to attract us to him, nothing in his appearance that we should desire him.

3) He was despised and rejected by men, a man of sorrows, and familiar with suffering. Like one from whom men hide their faces he was despised, and we esteemed him not.

4) *Surely he took up our infirmities and carried our sorrows,* yet we considered him stricken by God, smitten by him, and afflicted.

5) *But he was pierced for our transgressions, he was crushed for our iniquities; the punishment that brought us peace was upon him, and by his wounds we are healed.*

6) *We all, like sheep, have gone astray, each of us has turned to his own way; and the LORD has laid on him the iniquity of us all.*

7) He was oppressed and afflicted, yet he did not open his mouth; he was led like a lamb to the slaughter, and as a sheep before her shearers is silent, so he did not open his mouth.

8) By oppression and judgment he was taken away. And

who can speak of his descendants? For he was cut off from the land of the living; *for the transgression of my people he was stricken.*

9) He was assigned a grave with the wicked, and with the rich in his death, though he had done no violence, nor was any deceit in his mouth.

10) Yet it was the LORD's will to crush him and cause him to suffer, *and though the LORD makes his life a guilt offering,* he will see his offspring and prolong his days, and the will of the LORD will prosper in his hand.

11) After the suffering of his soul, he will see the light of life and be satisfied; *by his knowledge my righteous servant will justify many, and he will bear their iniquities.*

12) Therefore I will give him a portion among the great, and he will divide the spoils with the strong, because he poured out his life unto death, and was numbered with the transgressors. *For he bore the sin of many, and made intercession for the transgressors.*

(a remarkable prophecy of Christ's purpose for coming to earth, written approximately 700 years before he was born...God's Spirit speaking through Isaiah)

Luke 24:46-47

46) He told them, "This is what is written: The Christ will suffer and rise from the dead on the third day,

47) *and repentance and forgiveness of sins will be preached in his name to all nations, beginning at Jerusalem.*

John 6:51

51) I am the living bread that came down from heaven. If anyone eats of this bread, he will live forever. This bread is my flesh, *which I will give for the life of the world."*

John 10:14-15

14) "I am the good shepherd; I know my sheep and my sheep know me—

15) just as the Father knows me and I know the Father— *and I lay down my life for the sheep.*

Rom 5:8-10

8) *But God demonstrates his own love for us in this: While we were still sinners, Christ died for us.*

9) Since we have now been justified by his blood, how much more shall we be saved from God's wrath through him!

10) *For if, when we were God's enemies, we were reconciled to him through the death of his Son, how much more, having been reconciled, shall we be saved through his life!*

2Cor 5:20-21

20) We are therefore Christ's ambassadors, as though God were making his appeal through us. We implore you on Christ's behalf: *Be reconciled to God.*

21) *God made him who had no sin to be sin for us, so that in him we might become the righteousness of God.*

Gal 1:3-4

3) Grace and peace to you from God our Father and the Lord Jesus Christ,

4) *who gave himself for our sins to rescue us from the present evil age,* according to the will of our God and Father,

Eph 2:8-10

8) *For it is by grace you have been saved, through faith—and this not from yourselves, it is the gift of God—*

9) *not by works, so that no one can boast.*

10) For we are God's workmanship, created in Christ Jesus to do good works, which God prepared in advance for us to do.

(we do not gain salvation by "being good" in order to *earn* God's favor. *Only accepting God's gift of the blood of Christ shed on our behalf purifies us in his eyes. After* realizing this truth, *then* we are to gratefully make good deeds a part of our lives)

Col 1:13-14

13) *For he has rescued us from the dominion of darkness and brought us into the kingdom of the Son he loves,*

14) *in whom we have redemption, the forgiveness of sins.*

Heb 2:9-10

9) But we see Jesus, who was made a little lower than the angels, *now crowned with glory and honor because he suffered death, so that by the grace of God he might taste death for everyone.*

10) In bringing many sons to glory, it was fitting that God, for whom and through whom everything exists, should make the author of their salvation perfect through suffering.

1Pet 2:21-24

21) To this you were called, because Christ suffered for you, leaving you an example, that you should follow in his steps.

22) "He committed no sin, and no deceit was found in his mouth."

23) When they hurled their insults at him, he did not

retaliate; when he suffered, he made no threats. Instead, he entrusted himself to him who judges justly.

24) He himself bore our sins in his body on the tree, so that we might die to sins and live for righteousness; by his wounds you have been healed.

Heb 5:7-9

7) During the days of Jesus' life on earth, he offered up prayers and petitions with loud cries and tears to the one who could save him from death, and he was heard because of his reverent submission.

8) Although he was a son, he learned obedience from what he suffered

9) and, once made perfect, he became the source of eternal salvation for all who obey him

Heb 10:7-10

7) Then I said, 'Here I am—it is written about me in the scroll— I have come to do your will, O God.'"

8) First he said, "Sacrifices and offerings, burnt offerings and sin offerings you did not desire, nor were you pleased with them" (although the law required them to be made).

9) Then he said, "Here I am, I have come to do your will." He sets aside the first to establish the second.

10) And by that will, we have been made holy through the sacrifice of the body of Jesus Christ once for all.

(speaks about Old Testament law and animal sacrifices being replaced by New Testament grace and blood-of-Christ, whose obedient sacrifice was "once for all" the world, and final)

1John 4:9-10

9) This is how God showed his love among us: He sent his one and only Son into the world that we might live through him.

10) *This is love: not that we loved God, but that he loved us and sent his Son as an atoning sacrifice for our sins.*

*Note: *italics* added to relate to topic title; author comments in parentheses to clarify

Confess and Forsake

Ezek 18:23

23) Do I take any pleasure in the death of the wicked? declares the Sovereign LORD. *Rather, am I not pleased when they turn from their ways and live?*

Ezek 18:31-32

31) Rid yourselves of all the offenses you have committed, and get a new heart and a new spirit. Why will you die, O house of Israel?

32) For I take no pleasure in the death of anyone, declares the Sovereign LORD. Repent and live!

Isa 55:6-7

6) Seek the LORD while he may be found; call on him while he is near.

7) Let the wicked forsake his way and the evil man his thoughts. *Let him turn to the LORD, and he will have mercy on him, and to our God, for he will freely pardon.*

Prov 28:13

13) He who conceals his sins does not prosper, *but whoever confesses and renounces* them finds mercy.

Jer 18:11-12

11) "Now therefore say to the people of Judah and those living in Jerusalem, 'This is what the LORD says: Look! I am preparing a disaster for you and devising a plan against you. So turn from your evil ways, each one of you, and reform your ways and your actions.'

12) But they will reply, *'It's no use. We will continue with our own plans; each of us will follow the stubbornness of his evil heart.'"*

Rom 2:5

5) *But because of your stubbornness and your unrepentant heart, you are storing up wrath against yourself* for the day of God's wrath, when his righteous judgment will be revealed.

Mat 7:13-14

13) "Enter through the narrow gate. For wide is the gate and broad is the road that leads to destruction, *and many enter through it.*

14) But small is the gate and narrow the road that leads to life, *and only a few find it.*

John 8:10-11

10) Jesus straightened up and asked her, "Woman, where are they? Has no one condemned you?"

11) "No one, sir," she said. *"Then neither do I condemn you," Jesus declared. "Go now and leave your life of sin."*

Rom 8:7-9

7) the sinful mind is hostile to God. It does not submit to God's law, nor can it do so.

8) *Those controlled by the sinful nature cannot please God.*

9) You, however, are controlled not by the sinful nature but by the Spirit, if the Spirit of God lives in you. And

if anyone does not have the Spirit of Christ, he does not belong to Christ.

Rom 8:12-14

12) Therefore, brothers, we have an obligation—but it is not to the sinful nature, to live according to it.

13) *For if you live according to the sinful nature, you will die; but if by the Spirit you put to death the misdeeds of the body, you will live,*

14) because those who are led by the Spirit of God are sons of God.

Act 3:19

19) *Repent, then, and turn to God, so that your sins may be wiped out, that times of refreshing may come from the Lord,*

1Cor 6:18-20

18) Flee from sexual immorality. All other sins a man commits are outside his body, but he who sins sexually sins against his own body.

19) *Do you not know that your body is a temple of the Holy Spirit, who is in you, whom you have received from God? You are not your own;*

20) you were bought at a price. Therefore honor God with your body.

Rom 12:1-2

1) Therefore, I urge you, brothers, in view of God's mercy, to offer your bodies as living sacrifices, holy and pleasing to God—this is your spiritual act of worship.

2) *Do not conform any longer to the pattern of this world, but be transformed by the renewing of your mind.* Then you will be able to test and approve what God's will is—his good, pleasing and perfect will.

Gal 2:20

20) *I have been crucified with Christ and I no longer live, but Christ lives in me.* The life I live in the body, I live by faith in the Son of God, who loved me and gave himself for me.

Gal 6:7-8

7) *Do not be deceived: God cannot be mocked. A man reaps what he sows.*
8) The one who sows to please his sinful nature, from that nature will reap destruction; the one who sows to please the Spirit, from the Spirit will reap eternal life.

Col 3:5-10

5) *Put to death, therefore, whatever belongs to your earthly nature:* sexual immorality, impurity, lust, evil desires and greed, which is idolatry.
6) Because of these, the wrath of God is coming.
7) You used to walk in these ways, in the life you once lived.

8) *But now you must rid yourselves of all such things as these:* anger, rage, malice, slander, and filthy language from your lips.
9) *Do not lie to each other, since you have taken off your old self with its practices*
10) and have put on the new self, which is being renewed in knowledge in the image of its Creator.

Heb 10:26-27

26) If we deliberately keep on sinning after we have received the knowledge of the truth, *no sacrifice for sins is left,*
27) but only a fearful expectation of judgment and of raging fire that will consume the enemies of God.

1Pet 1:13-14

13) Therefore, prepare your minds for action; be self-controlled; set your hope fully on the grace to be given you when Jesus Christ is revealed.

14) *As obedient children, do not conform to the evil desires you had when you lived in ignorance.*

2Pet 1:5-10

5) For this very reason, make every effort to add to your faith goodness; and to goodness, knowledge;

6) and to knowledge, self-control; and to self-control, perseverance; and to perseverance, godliness;

7) and to godliness, brotherly kindness; and to brotherly kindness, love.

8) *For if you possess these qualities in increasing measure, they will keep you from being ineffective and unproductive in your knowledge of our Lord Jesus Christ.*

9) *But if anyone does not have them, he is nearsighted and blind, and has forgotten that he has been cleansed from his past sins.*

10) Therefore, my brothers, be all the more eager to make your calling and election sure. For if you do these things, you will never fall,

Rev 3:15-17

15) I know your deeds, that you are neither cold nor hot. I wish you were either one or the other!

16) *So, because you are lukewarm—neither hot nor cold—I am about to spit you out of my mouth.*

17) You say, 'I am rich; I have acquired wealth and do not need a thing.' *But you do not realize that you are wretched, pitiful, poor, blind and naked.*

*Note: *italics* added to relate to topic title; author comments in parentheses to clarify

What God requires of Mankind

Mic 6:8

8) He has showed you, O man, what is good. And what does the LORD require of you? *To act* justly *and to love mercy and to walk humbly with your God.*

Deut 5:29

29) Oh, that their hearts would be inclined to fear me and keep all my commands always, so that it might go well with them and their children forever!

Deut 13:4

4) It is the LORD your God you must follow, and him you must revere. Keep his commands and obey him; serve him and hold fast to him.

Prov 1:7

7) *The fear of the LORD is the beginning of knowledge, but fools despise wisdom and* discipline.

(fear of the LORD = respect, honor, willingness to submit to a Higher Power)

Eccl 12:13

13) Now all has been heard; here is the conclusion of the matter: *Fear God and keep his commandments, for this is the whole duty of man.*

1Sam 16:7

7) But the LORD said to Samuel, "Do not consider his appearance or his height, for I have rejected him. The LORD does not look at the things man looks at. *Man looks at the outward appearance, but the LORD looks at the heart."*

Exo 19:5-6

5) *Now if you obey me fully and keep my covenant, then out of all nations you will be my treasured possession. Although the whole earth is mine,*
6) *you will be for me a kingdom of priests and a holy nation.'* These are the words you are to speak to the Israelites."

(we know the Israelites eventually failed in their allegiance, and were forsaken by God when the Romans destroyed their nation in 70 A.D. Today, these words are for true Believers in Christ all around the world, whether of Jewish descent or from other nations, the Gentiles)

Luke 10:25-28

25) On one occasion an expert in the law stood up to test Jesus. "Teacher," he asked "what must I do to inherit eternal life?"
26) "What is written in the Law?" he replied. "How do you read it?"
27) He answered: *"Love the Lord your God with all your heart and with all your soul and with all your strength and with all your mind'; and, 'Love your neighbor as yourself.'"*
28) "You have answered correctly," Jesus replied. *"Do this and you will live."*

Jam 1:25

25) But the man who looks intently into the perfect law
    that gives freedom, and continues to do this, not
    forgetting what he has heard, *but doing it*—he will
    be blessed in what he does.

(next 2 entries explain what *"doing it"* means; an ongo-
ing, lifetime learning process)

1Cor 13:1-7

1) If I speak in the tongues of men and of angels, *but
   have not love*, I am only a resounding gong or a
   clanging cymbal.
2) If I have the gift of prophecy and can fathom all
   mysteries and all knowledge, and if I have a faith that
   can move mountains, *but have not love*, I am nothing.
3) If I give all I possess to the poor and surrender my
   body to the flames, *but have not love*, I gain nothing.

4) *Love is patient, love is kind. It does not envy, it does
   not boast, it is not proud.*
5) *It is not rude, it is not self-seeking, it is not easily
   angered, it keeps no record of wrongs.*
6) *Love does not delight in evil but rejoices with the
   truth.*
7) *It always protects, always trusts, always hopes,
   always perseveres.*

(describes a gentle, unselfish spirit...at peace through
feeling forgiven/accepted by God)

Gal 5:16-24

16) So I say, live by the Spirit, and you will not gratify the
    desires of the sinful nature.
17) *For the sinful nature desires what is contrary to the
    Spirit, and the Spirit what is contrary to the sinful
    nature. They are in conflict with each other, so that
    you do not do what you want.*

18) But if you are led by the Spirit, you are not under law.

19) *The acts of the sinful nature are obvious:* sexual immorality, impurity and debauchery;
20) idolatry and witchcraft; hatred, discord, jealousy, fits of rage, selfish ambition, dissensions, factions
21) and envy; drunkenness, orgies, and the like. I warn you, as I did before, that those who live like this will not inherit the kingdom of God.

22) *But the fruit of the Spirit is love, joy, peace, patience, kindness, goodness, faithfulness,*
23) *gentleness and self-control. Against such things there is no law.*
24) Those who belong to Christ Jesus have crucified the sinful nature with its passions and desires.

(remember, the "fruit of the Spirit" takes time to learn; God is patient and forgiving)

Php 2:12-15

12) Therefore, my dear friends, as you have always obeyed—not only in my presence, but now much more in my absence—continue to work out your salvation with fear and trembling,
13) for it is God who works in you to will and to act according to his good purpose.
14) Do everything without complaining or arguing,
15) *so that you may become blameless and pure, children of God without fault in a crooked and depraved generation, in which you shine like stars in the universe*

Gal 6:1

1) Brothers, if someone is caught in a sin, you who are spiritual should restore him gently. *But watch yourself, or you also may be tempted.*

1Cor 10:13

13) No temptation has seized you except what is common to man. And God is faithful; *he will not let you be tempted beyond what you can bear.* But when you are tempted, *he will also provide a way out so that you can stand up under it.*

(in this fallen-from-grace world we live in, it is impossible to not be tempted into wrongdoings *daily, even hour by hour*. But the Scriptures encourage us to persevere, and God will help us withstand it)

*Note: *italics* added to relate to topic title; author comments in parentheses to clarify

How to know
the invisible God personally

Act 17:24-27

24) "The God who made the world and everything in it is the Lord of heaven and earth and does not live in temples built by hands.

25) *And he is not served by human hands, as if he needed anything, because he himself gives all men life and breath and everything else.*

26) From one man he made every nation of men, that they should inhabit the whole earth; and he determined the times set for them and the exact places where they should live.

27) *God did this so that men would seek him and perhaps reach out for him and find him, though he is not far from each one of us.*

(all people are "bubble-wrapped", so to speak, by God's invisible Spirit every moment of every day. Each breath we take the unseen Spirit is both inside and outside our bodies and minds, because he is able to literally be everywhere at the same time. Psa 139:1-14 describes some of God's unlimited powers)

John 1:18

18) No one has ever seen God, but God the One and Only, who is at the Father's side, *has made him known.*

(for about 33 years God was visible on this earth in a physical human body. Look to Christ in order to "see" God...he was the only person ever to be conceived by God's Spirit. see Luke 1: 35)

Rev 3:20

20) Here I am! I stand at the door and knock. *If anyone hears my voice and opens the door, I will come in and eat with him, and he with me.*

(we must first acknowledge the Spirit's "small, still voice" nudging our consciences as God reveals the need for forgiveness within, and draws us to Christ over time) see next entry.

John 6:44

44) "No one can come to me *unless the Father who sent me draws him*, and I will raise him up at the last day.

Eph 2:22

22) And in him you too are being built together to become a dwelling in which God lives by his Spirit.

(we gradually grow to recognize God's Spirit through his gentle prodding inside our consciences)

John 4:24

24) God is spirit, and his worshipers must worship in spirit and in truth."

John 14:16-21

16) And I will ask the Father, and he will give you another Counselor to be with you forever—

17) *the Spirit of truth.* The world cannot accept him, because it neither sees him nor knows him. But you know him, *for he lives with you and will be in you.*

18) I will not leave you as orphans; *I will come to you.*
19) Before long, the world will not see me anymore, but you will see me. Because I live, you also will live.
20) On that day you will realize that I am in my Father, and you are in me, and I am in you.
21) *Whoever has my commands and obeys them, he is the one who loves me. He who loves me will be loved by my Father, and I too will love him and show myself to him."*

(for anyone doing his/her best to bring their lifestyle and behavior in line with the Scriptures, even though we cannot be perfect like Christ, God's Spirit will "show himself")

John 6:45
45) It is written in the Prophets: *'They will all be taught by God.'* Everyone who listens to the Father and learns from him comes to me.

(we learn from the Scriptures, his Spirit's guidance in our consciences, yes-or-no answers to prayer, and daily circumstances that happen as we interact with other people)

2Tim 3:16-17
16) *All Scripture is God-breathed and is useful for teaching, rebuking, correcting and training in righteousness,*
17) so that the man of God may be thoroughly equipped for every good work.

Heb 11:6
6) And without faith it is impossible to please God, because anyone who comes to him must believe that he exists and that *he rewards those who earnestly seek him.*

Psa 145:18
18) The LORD is near to all who call on him, *to all who call on him in truth.*

Jam 4:8

8) *Come near to God and he will come near to you.*
Wash your hands, you sinners, and purify your
hearts, you double-minded.

1John 2:27

27) As for you, *the anointing you received from him
remains in you,* and you do not need anyone to
teach you. But as his anointing teaches you about all
things and as that anointing is real, not counterfeit—
just as it has taught you, remain in him.

(the word "counterfeit" reminds us it is critical to remember 1John 4:1-2, which speaks about testing the Spirits and being on guard against false prophets)

1Cor 2:12-14

12) *We have not received the spirit of the world but the
Spirit who is from God, that we may understand
what God has freely given us.*

13) This is what we speak, not in words taught us by
human wisdom but in words taught by the Spirit,
expressing spiritual truths in spiritual words.

14) *The man without the Spirit does not accept the
things that come from the Spirit of God, for they are
foolishness to him, and he cannot understand them,
because they are spiritually discerned.*

*Note: *italics* added to relate to topic title; author
comments in parentheses to clarify

Principles for daily life

Josh 1:8

8) Do not let this Book of the Law depart from your mouth; *meditate on it day and night,* so that you may be careful to do everything written in it. Then you will be prosperous and successful.

(today, Christians are not required to keep all the pre-Christ Old Testament ceremonial rules and guilt offerings that the Israelites of old were. But we are charged with learning God's principles and the world history laid out in the Old Testament, as well as becoming doers of God's Word as taught in the New Testament)

Psa 1:1-3

1) Blessed is the man who does not walk in the counsel of the wicked or stand in the way of sinners or sit in the seat of mockers.
2) *But his delight is in the law of the LORD,* and on his law he meditates day and night.
3) He is like a tree planted by streams of water, which yields its fruit in season and whose leaf does not wither. *Whatever he does prospers.*

Psa 86:11

11) Teach me your way, O LORD, and I will walk in your truth; give me an undivided heart, *that I may fear your name.*

("fear your name" = respect, honor, willingness to submit to a Higher Power)

Mic 6:8

8) He has showed you, O man, what is good. And what does the LORD require of you? *To act justly and to love mercy and to walk humbly with your God.*

Psa 32:8-9

8) *I will instruct you and teach you in the way you should go; I will counsel you and watch over you.*

9) Do not be like the horse or the mule, which have no understanding but must be controlled by bit and bridle or they will not come to you.

(many of us are too strong-willed to submit to God's principles. We want to be in charge of our lifestyles, pleasures, and decisions—without outside guidelines or authority. However, such temporary "self-service" can carry a heavy penalty) see next entry.

Rom 2:6-8

6) God "will give to each person according to what he has done."

7) To those who by persistence in doing good seek glory, honor and immortality, *he will give eternal life.*

8) *But for those who are self-seeking and who reject the truth and follow evil, there will be wrath and anger*

Mat 18:1-4

1) At that time the disciples came to Jesus and asked, "Who is the greatest in the kingdom of heaven?"

2) He called a little child and had him stand among them.

3) And he said: "I tell you the truth, unless you change and become like little children, you will never enter the kingdom of heaven.

4) Therefore, whoever humbles himself like this child is the greatest in the kingdom of heaven.

(be willing to look up to almighty God as our Father-figure. It's just that simple)

John 3:30-31

30) He must become greater; I must become less.

31) "The one who comes from above is above all; the one who is from the earth belongs to the earth, and speaks as one from the earth. The one who comes from heaven is above all.

John 15:10

10) *If you obey my commands, you will remain in my love,* just as I have obeyed my Father's commands and remain in his love.

Php 2:14-15

14) Do everything without complaining or arguing,

15) so that you may become blameless and pure, *children of God without fault in a crooked and depraved generation, in which you shine like stars in the universe*

Mat 6:19-21

19) "Do not store up for yourselves treasures on earth, where moth and rust destroy, and where thieves break in and steal.

20) But store up for yourselves treasures in heaven, where moth and rust do not destroy, and where thieves do not break in and steal.

21) *For where your treasure is, there your heart will be also.*

1Tim 6:10

10) For the *love of money* is a root of all kinds of evil. Some people, *eager for money*, have wandered from the faith and pierced themselves with many griefs.

Prov 16:2

2) All a man's ways seem innocent to him, *but motives are weighed by the LORD.*

Rom 12:17-21

17) *Do not repay anyone evil for evil.* Be careful to do what is right in the eyes of everybody.

18) If it is possible, as far as it depends on you, live at peace with everyone.

19) *Do not take revenge, my friends, but leave room for God's wrath, for it is written: "It is mine to avenge; I will repay," says the Lord.*

20) On the contrary: "If your enemy is hungry, feed him; if he is thirsty, give him something to drink. *In doing this, you will heap burning coals on his head."*

21) Do not be overcome by evil, but overcome evil with good.

Jam 3:13-17

13) *Who is wise and understanding among you? Let him show it by his good life, by deeds done in the humility that comes from wisdom.*

14) But if you harbor bitter envy and selfish ambition in your hearts, do not boast about it or deny the truth.

15) Such "wisdom" does not come down from heaven but is earthly, unspiritual, of the devil.

16) For where you have envy and selfish ambition, there you find disorder and every evil practice.

17) *But the wisdom that comes from heaven is first of all pure; then peace-loving, considerate, submissive, full of mercy and good fruit, impartial and sincere.*

Rom 13:9-10

9) The commandments, "Do not commit adultery," "Do not murder," "Do not steal," "Do not covet," and whatever other commandment there may be, are summed up in this one rule: *"Love your neighbor as yourself."*

10) Love does no harm to its neighbor. *Therefore love is the fulfillment of the law.*

Luke 6:31

31) Do to others as you would have them do to you.

Eph 4:1-3

1) As a prisoner for the Lord, then, I urge you to live a life worthy of the calling you have received.
2) *Be completely humble and gentle; be patient, bearing with one another in love.*
3) Make every effort to keep the unity of the Spirit through the bond of peace.

Tit 3:3-5

3) *At one time we too were foolish, disobedient, deceived and enslaved by all kinds of passions and pleasures. We lived in malice and envy, being hated and hating one another.*
4) But when the kindness and love of God our Savior appeared,
5) he saved us, *not because of righteous things we had done, but because of his mercy.* He saved us through the washing of rebirth and renewal by the Holy Spirit,

1Pet 1:14 & 17-19

14) As obedient children, do not conform to the evil desires you had when you lived in ignorance...

...17) Since you call on a Father who judges each man's work impartially, *live your lives as strangers here in reverent fear.*
18) For you know that it was not with perishable things such as silver or gold that you were *redeemed from the empty way of life handed down to you from your forefathers,*

19) but with the precious blood of Christ, a lamb without blemish or defect.

Jam 3:6-10

6) The tongue also is a fire, a world of evil among the parts of the body. *It corrupts the whole person,* sets the whole course of his life on fire, and is itself set on fire by hell.

7) All kinds of animals, birds, reptiles and creatures of the sea are being tamed and have been tamed by man,

8) *but no man can tame the tongue.* It is a restless evil, full of deadly poison.

9) With the tongue we praise our Lord and Father, and with it we curse men, who have been made in God's likeness.

10) *Out of the same mouth come praise and cursing. My brothers, this should not be.*

*Note: *italics* added to relate to topic title; author comments in parentheses to clarify

Forgiveness - judging others

Rom 14:1-6

1) Accept him whose faith is weak, *without passing judgment on disputable matters.*

2) One man's faith allows him to eat everything, but another man, whose faith is weak, eats only vegetables.

3) The man who eats everything must not look down on him who does not, and the man who does not eat everything must not condemn the man who does, for God has accepted him.

4) *Who are you to judge someone else's servant?* To his own master he stands or falls. And he will stand, for the Lord is able to make him stand.

5) One man considers one day more sacred than another; another man considers every day alike. *Each one should be fully convinced in his own mind.*

6) He who regards one day as special, does so to the Lord. He who eats meat, eats to the Lord, for he gives thanks to God; and he who abstains, does so to the Lord and gives thanks to God.

Rom 14:10-13

10) You, then, why do you judge your brother? Or why do you look down on your brother? For we will all stand before God's judgment seat.

11) It is written: "'As surely as I live,' says the Lord, "every knee will bow before me; every tongue will confess to God.'"

12) So then, each of us will give an account of himself to God.

13) *Therefore let us stop passing judgment on one another. Instead, make up your mind not to put any stumbling block or obstacle in your brother's way.*

Col 2:16-17

16) *Therefore do not let anyone judge you* by what you eat or drink, or with regard to a religious festival, a New Moon celebration or a Sabbath day.

17) These are a shadow of the things that were to come; *the reality, however, is found in Christ.*

(other sometimes contentious debates by both sides have included: baptism required for salvation, banning wine and strong drink completely, artificial birth- control, speaking in tongues, abortion, homosexuality, different kinds of music, dancing, card games, etc.

We all need to remember that other people are at different stages of maturity in their knowledge of God, or lack of it, than we are; either not convinced yet their lifestyles need to change, or holding onto their right to choose not to change at any point in time.

Others do not have the exact same background we do, and as the above verse states, *the reality is found in Christ*— we do not *earn salvation* on the "B.C." side of the cross. Lifestyle changes are to come "A.D.", *after* accepting the forgiveness God offers through Christ, and not until God's Spirit convinces people *inside their hearts* to change.

Truly, all people are fortunate to have an understanding God as our judge instead of human beings, who are more critical and much less patient with our fellow man. While it's true some people stubbornly insist on testing God by demanding their own way, others may simply be untaught/unaware, or worse, misguided by someone's non-biblical teaching)

Rom 14:22

22) *So whatever you believe about these things keep between yourself and God. Blessed is the man who does not condemn himself by what he approves.*

Luke 6:37-38

37) *"Do not judge, and you will not be judged. Do not condemn, and you will not be condemned. Forgive, and you will be forgiven.*

38) Give, and it will be given to you. A good measure, pressed down, shaken together and running over, will be poured into your lap. *For with the measure you use, it will be measured to you."*

(these verses are meaningful for all of us; Mat 7:1-5 has more truth on harsh judgments)

Prov 24:29

29) Do not say, "I'll do to him as he has done to me; I'll pay that man back for what he did."

Mat 5:7

7) *Blessed are the merciful, for they will be shown mercy.*

John 8:7

7) When they kept on questioning him, he straightened up and said to them, *"If any one of you is without sin, let him be the first to throw a stone at her."*

Jam 4:11-12

11) *Brothers, do not slander one another.* Anyone who speaks against his brother or judges him speaks against the law and judges it. When you judge the law, you are not keeping it, but sitting in judgment on it.

12) *There is only one Lawgiver and Judge, the one who is able to save and destroy.* But you—who are you to judge your neighbor?

Prov 10:18

18) He who conceals his hatred has lying lips, and *whoever spreads slander is a fool.*

Col 3:12-15

12) Therefore, as God's chosen people, holy and dearly loved, *clothe yourselves with compassion, kindness, humility, gentleness and patience.*

13) Bear with each other and forgive whatever grievances you may have against one another. *Forgive as the Lord forgave you.*

14) And over all these virtues put on love, which binds them all together in perfect unity.

15) Let the peace of Christ rule in your hearts, since as members of one body you were called to peace. And be thankful.

Eph 4:30-32

30) And do not grieve the Holy Spirit of God, with whom you were sealed for the day of redemption.

31) Get rid of all bitterness, rage and anger, brawling and slander, along with every form of malice.

32) Be kind and compassionate to one another, *forgiving each other, just as in Christ God forgave you.*

1Tim 1:12-16

12) I thank Christ Jesus our Lord, who has given me strength, that he considered me faithful, appointing me to his service.

13) Even though I was once a blasphemer and a persecutor and a violent man, *I was shown mercy because I acted in ignorance and unbelief.*

14) The grace of our Lord was poured out on me abundantly, along with the faith and love that are in Christ Jesus.

15) Here is a trustworthy saying that deserves full acceptance: *Christ Jesus came into the world to save sinners—of whom I am the worst.*

16) *But for that very reason I was shown mercy so that in me, the worst of sinners, Christ Jesus might display his unlimited patience as an example for those who would believe on him and receive eternal life.*

(he who is forgiven much, *and knows it,* can more easily forgive others of their faults)

1Sam 16:7

7) But the LORD said to Samuel, "Do not consider his appearance or his height, for I have rejected him. The LORD does not look at the things man looks at. *Man looks at the outward appearance, but the LORD looks at the heart.*"

*Note: *italics* added to relate to topic title; author comments in parentheses to clarify

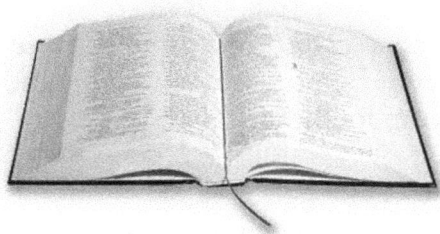

Prayer guidelines

Dan 10:12

12) Then he continued, "Do not be afraid, Daniel. *Since the first day that you set your mind to gain understanding and to humble yourself before your God,* your words were heard, and I have come in response to them.

("humble" = the opposite of self-pride and egotism; unpretentious)

Jam 4:10

10) *Humble yourselves before the Lord,* and he will lift you up.

Heb 10:22

22) *let us draw near to God with a sincere heart in full assurance of faith,* having our hearts sprinkled to cleanse us from a guilty conscience and having our bodies washed with pure water.

Jer 29:13

13) You will seek me and find me *when you seek me with all your heart.*

(we must first sincerely want to know God; he will not force himself on anyone)

Jam 4:8

8) *Come near to God and he will come near to you.* Wash your hands, you sinners, and purify your hearts, you double-minded.

1John 5:14

14) This is the confidence we have in approaching God: *that if we ask anything according to his will, he hears us.* (see entry below)

Luke 22:42

42) "Father, if you are willing, take this cup from me; *yet not my will, but yours be done.*"

(only God knows what is best for each individual in order to fit into his far-reaching plans. Sometimes his answer is simply "no", or perhaps "not now, but later". Even Christ *left it with God the Father* in the verse above)

2Cor 12:8-9

8) Three times I pleaded with the Lord to take it away from me.

9) But he said to me, *"My grace is sufficient for you, for my power is made perfect in weakness."* Therefore I will boast all the more gladly about my weaknesses, so that Christ's power may rest on me.

(weakness often draws us closer to God, making us need his help, which he loves to give. Very important we understand "not my will, but yours be done") see entry above and below.

Rom 8:26-28

26) In the same way, the Spirit helps us in our weakness. *We do not know what we ought to pray for, but the Spirit himself intercedes for us with groans that words cannot express.*

27) And he who searches our hearts knows the mind of the Spirit, because the Spirit intercedes for the saints in accordance with God's will.

28) *And we know that in all things God works for the good of those who love him, who have been called according to his purpose.*

(leave it with God—*then wait*—days or weeks if necessary, so his Spirit has time to Work through people near or far if needed. Whether he answers yes or no, it will work out for good in the end)

Php 4:6-7

6) *Do not be anxious about anything,* but in everything, by prayer and petition, with thanksgiving, present your requests to God.

7) And the peace of God, which transcends all understanding, will guard your hearts and your minds in Christ Jesus.

(read and re-read Rom 8:26-28 above to learn how to "not be anxious about anything")

1John 3:21-23

21) Dear friends, if our hearts do not condemn us, we have confidence before God

22) *and receive from him anything we ask, because we obey his commands and do what pleases him.*

23) *And this is his command: to believe in the name of his Son, Jesus Christ, and to love one another as he commanded us.*

(as stated, to "receive from him anything we ask" we must first "obey his commands and do what pleases him", which means accepting Christ as our substitute in payment for our wrongdoings, *plus* applying principles such as Gal 5:16-26 and 1 Cor chap. 13 into our daily lives as we gradually grow in faith)

John 15:7

7) *If you remain in me and my words remain in you,* ask whatever you wish, and it will be given you.

(remember "if my words remain in you". Digesting the Bible is the main way to learn about God, and how to pray in his will. Get into the New Testament first; daily is best)

John 9:31

31) We know that God does not listen to sinners. *He listens to the godly man who does his will.*

(none of us can be perfect, but we must be *sincere*. After receiving Christ, God is patient with our mistakes if we *do our best* to overcome the old, selfish nature)

Psa 66:18

18) *If I had cherished sin in my heart*, the Lord would not have listened;

(we must give up old attitudes and habits we cling to, *of which we know God disapproves*, or he will not hear) see entry below.

Isa 59:2

2) But your iniquities have *separated you from your God*; your sins have hidden his face from you, *so that he will not hear.*

Jam 4:1-4

1) What causes fights and quarrels among you? Don't they come from your desires that battle within you?
2) You want something but don't get it. You kill and covet, but you cannot have what you want. You quarrel and fight. *You do not have, because you do not ask God.*
3) When you ask, you do not receive, *because you ask with wrong motives, that you may spend what you get on your pleasures.*

4) You adulterous people, don't you know that friendship with the world is hatred toward God? *Anyone who chooses to be a friend of the world becomes an enemy of God.*

Mat 6:5-8

5) "And when you pray, *do not be like the hypocrites,* for they love to pray standing in the synagogues and on the street corners *to be seen by men.* I tell you the truth, they have received their reward in full.

6) But when you pray, go into your room, close the door and pray to your Father, who is unseen. Then your Father, *who sees what is done in secret,* will reward you.

7) *And when you pray, do not keep on babbling like pagans, for they think they will be heard because of their many words.*

8) Do not be like them, for your Father knows what you need before you ask him

*Note: *italics* added to relate to topic title; author comments in parentheses to clarify

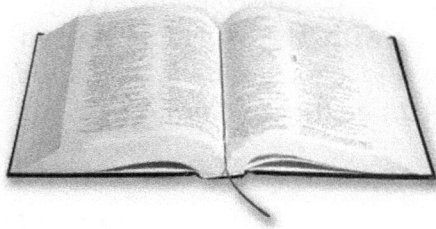

Faith and Trust - promises of God

2Pet 1:3-4

3) His divine power has given us everything we need for life and godliness through our knowledge of him who called us by his own glory and goodness.

4) *Through these he has given us his very great and precious promises, so that through them you may participate in the divine nature and escape the corruption in the world caused by evil desires.*

Psa 103:8-12

8) The LORD is compassionate and gracious, slow to anger, abounding in love.

9) He will not always accuse, nor will he harbor his anger forever;

10) *he does not treat us as our sins deserve or repay us according to our iniquities.*

11) For as high as the heavens are above the earth, *so great is his love for those who fear him;*

12) as far as the east is from the west, so far has he removed our transgressions from us.

Psa 9:10

10) Those who know your name will trust in you, for you, LORD, *have never forsaken those who seek you.*

Isa 40:28-31

28) Do you not know? Have you not heard? The LORD is the everlasting God, the Creator of the ends of the earth. *He will not grow tired or weary,* and his understanding no one can fathom.

29) *He gives strength to the weary and increases the power of the weak.*

30) Even youths grow tired and weary, and young men stumble and fall;

31) *but those who hope in the LORD will renew their strength.* They will soar on wings like eagles; they will run and not grow weary, they will walk and not be faint.

Prov 3:5-6

5) *Trust in the LORD with all your heart and lean not on your own understanding;*

6) *in all your ways acknowledge him, and he will make your paths straight.*

Psa 23:1-6

1) The LORD is my shepherd, I shall not be in want.

2) He makes me lie down in green pastures, he leads me beside quiet waters,

3) he restores my soul. He guides me in paths of righteousness for his name's sake.

4) Even though I walk through the valley of the shadow of death, I will fear no evil, for you are with me; your rod and your staff, they comfort me.

5) You prepare a table before me in the presence of my enemies. You anoint my head with oil; my cup overflows.

6) Surely goodness and love will follow me all the days of my life, and I will dwell in the house of the LORD forever.

Isa 41:10

10) *So do not fear, for I am with you; do not be dismayed, for I am your God.* I will strengthen you and help you; I will uphold you with my righteous right hand.

Psa 37:7-11

7) *Be still before the LORD and wait patiently for him;* do not fret when men succeed in their ways, when they carry out their wicked schemes.

8) Refrain from anger and turn from wrath; do not fret—it leads only to evil.

9) For evil men will be cut off, but those who hope in the LORD will inherit the land.

10) *A little while, and the wicked will be no more; though you look for them, they will not be found.*

11) *But the meek will inherit the land and enjoy great peace.*

Psa 118:8

8) *It is better to take refuge in the LORD than to trust in man.*

Mat 6:31-34

31) So do not worry, saying, 'What shall we eat?' or 'What shall we drink?' or 'What shall we wear?'

32) For the pagans run after all these things, and your heavenly Father knows that you need them.

33) *But seek first his kingdom and his righteousness, and all these things will be given to you as well.*

34) Therefore do not worry about tomorrow, for tomorrow will worry about itself. Each day has enough trouble of its own.

John 16:33

33) "I have told you these things, so that in me you may have peace. *In this world you will have trouble. But take heart! I have overcome the world.*"

Mat 11:28-29

28) *"Come to me, all you who are weary and burdened, and I will give you rest.*

29) Take my yoke upon you and learn from me, *for I am gentle and humble in heart,* and you will find rest for your souls.

John 1:12-13

12) *Yet to all who received him, to those who believed in his name, he gave the right to become children of God—*

13) children born not of natural descent, nor of human decision or a husband's will, but born of God.

John 3:16

16) "For God so loved the world that he gave his one and only Son, *that whoever believes in him shall not perish but have eternal life.*

John 6:40

40) For my Father's will is that everyone who looks to the Son and believes in him shall have eternal life, *and I will raise him up at the last day."*

John 14:27

27) Peace I leave with you; my peace I give you. *I do not give to you as the world gives.* Do not let your hearts be troubled and do not be afraid.

Rom 8:28

28) *And we know that in all things God works for the good of those who love him,* who have been called according to his purpose.

Rom 8:35-39

35) *Who shall separate us from the love of Christ?* Shall trouble or hardship or persecution or famine or nakedness or danger or sword?

36) As it is written: "For your sake we face death all day long; we are considered as sheep to be slaughtered."

37) No, in all these things we are more than conquerors through him who loved us.

38) For I am convinced that neither death nor life, neither angels nor demons, neither the present nor the future, nor any powers,

39) neither height nor depth, nor anything else in all creation, will be able to separate us from the love of God that is in Christ Jesus our Lord.

Php 4:11-13

11) I am not saying this because I am in need, for *I have learned to be content whatever the circumstances.*

12) I know what it is to be in need, and I know what it is to have plenty. I have learned the secret of being content in any and every situation, whether well fed or hungry, whether living in plenty or in want.

13) I can do everything through him who gives me strength.

Heb 11:1

1) Now faith is being sure of what we hope for and certain of what we do not see.

Heb 11:6

6) And without faith it is impossible to please God, *because anyone who comes to him must believe that he exists and that he rewards those who earnestly seek him.*

*Note: *italics* added to relate to topic title; author comments in parentheses to clarify

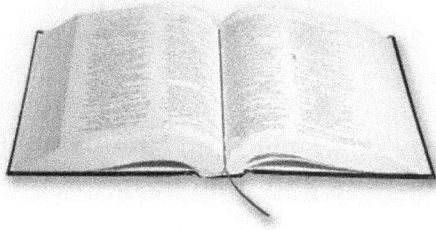

Life on earth temporary

Psa 103:13-16

13) As a father has compassion on his children, so the LORD has compassion on those who fear him;

14) for he knows how we are formed, he remembers that we are dust.

15) *As for man, his days are like grass, he flourishes like a flower of the field;*

16) *the wind blows over it and it is gone, and its place remembers it no more.*

Eccl 5:15-16

15) *Naked a man comes from his mother's womb, and as he comes, so he departs. He takes nothing from his labor that he can carry in his hand.*

16) This too is a grievous evil: As a man comes, so he departs, and what does he gain, since he toils for the wind?

Mat 16:24-27

24) Then Jesus said to his disciples, "If anyone would come after me, he must deny himself and take up his cross and follow me.

25) For whoever wants to save his life will lose it, but whoever loses his life for me will find it.

26) *What good will it be for a man if he gains the whole world, yet forfeits his soul? Or what can a man give in exchange for his soul?*

27) For the Son of Man is going to come in his Father's glory with his angels, and then he will reward each person according to what he has done.

1John 2:15-17

15) Do not love the world or anything in the world. If anyone loves the world, the love of the Father is not in him.

16) *For everything in the world—the cravings of sinful man, the lust of his eyes and the boasting of what he has and does—comes not from the Father but from the world.*

17) *The world and its desires pass away,* but the man who does the will of God lives forever.

(reveals how God views our seemingly endless pursuit of "pleasures and treasures")

1Tim 6:6-10

6)   But godliness with contentment is great gain.

7)   For we brought nothing into the world, and we can take nothing out of it.

8)   But if we have food and clothing, we will be content with that.

9)   *People who want to get rich fall into temptation and a trap and into many foolish* and harmful desires that plunge men into ruin and destruction.

10) For the *love of money* is a root of all kinds of evil. Some people, *eager for money*, have wandered from the faith and pierced themselves with many griefs.

(note it is not money itself that corrupts, but "love and eagerness" for money and all the possessions it will buy that corrupts our thinking. *Possessions are temporary,* and mistaken pride in the world's view of "success" can lead to a bloated ego)

1Pet 1:17
17) Since you call on a Father who judges each man's work impartially, *live your lives as strangers here in reverent fear.*

Job 14:1-2
1) "Man born of woman is of few days and full of trouble.
2) He springs up like a flower and withers away; like a fleeting shadow, he does not endure.

Heb 13:14
14) *For here we do not have an enduring city,* but we are looking for the city that is to come.

2Cor 4:18
18) So we fix our eyes not on what is seen, but on what is unseen. *For what is seen is temporary, but what is unseen is eternal.*

Col 3:1-2
1) Since, then, you have been raised with Christ, set your hearts on things above, where Christ is seated at the right hand of God.
2) *Set your minds on things above, not on earthly things.*

Php 3:7-8
7) But whatever was to my profit I now consider loss for the sake of Christ.
8) *What is more, I consider everything a loss compared to the surpassing greatness of knowing Christ Jesus my Lord, for whose sake I have lost all things. I consider them rubbish, that I may gain Christ*

Php 1:21-24
21) *For to me, to live is Christ and to die is gain.*

22) If I am to go on living in the body, this will mean fruitful labor for me. Yet what shall I choose? I do not know!
23) I am torn between the two: *I desire to depart and be with Christ, which is better by far;*
24) but it is more necessary for you that I remain in the body..

> (all Christians can take heart at these words above: "to die is gain" and "I desire to depart and be with Christ, which is better by far". We have a certain expectation that once these few trying years on earth pass, God has prepared a place for us beyond anything our minds can imagine. We can face the end with peace and hope...see 1Cor 2:9)

2Cor 5:6-10

6) Therefore we are always confident and know that as long as we are at home in the body we are away from the Lord.
7) We live by faith, not by sight.
8) *We are confident, I say, and would prefer to be away from the body and at home with the Lord.*
9) *So we make it our goal to please him,* whether we are at home in the body or away from it.
10) For we must all appear before the judgment seat of Christ, that each one may receive what is due him for the things done while in the body, whether good or bad.

Php 3:19-21

19) Their destiny is destruction, their god is their stomach, and their glory is in their shame. *Their mind is on earthly things.*
20) *But our citizenship is in heaven.* And we eagerly await a Savior from there, the Lord Jesus Christ,
21) who, by the power that enables him to bring everything under his control, *will transform our lowly bodies so that they will be like his glorious body.*

Php 4:12-13

12) I know what it is to be in need, and I know what it is to have plenty. *I have learned the secret of being content in any and every situation, whether well fed or hungry, whether living in plenty or in want.*

13) I can do everything through him who gives me strength.

Jam 4:13-16

13) Now listen, you who say, "Today or tomorrow we will go to this or that city, spend a year there, carry on business and make money."

14) Why, you do not even know what will happen tomorrow. What is your life? You are a mist that appears for a little while and then vanishes.

15) Instead, you ought to say, "If it is the Lord's will, we will live and do this or that."

16) As it is, you boast and brag. All such boasting is evil.

*Note: *italics* added to relate to topic title; author comments in parentheses to clarify

Trials and Tribulations

Rom 8:18-23

18) I consider that our present sufferings are not worth comparing with the glory that will be revealed in us.
19) The creation waits in eager expectation for the sons of God to be revealed.
20) *For the creation was subjected to frustration, not by its own choice, but by the will of the one who subjected it, in hope*
21) *that the creation itself will be liberated from its bondage to decay and brought into the glorious freedom of the children of God.*
22) We know that the whole creation has been groaning as in the pains of childbirth right up to the present time.
23) Not only so, but we ourselves, who have the firstfruits of the Spirit, groan inwardly as we wait eagerly for our adoption as sons, the redemption of our bodies.

Rom 5:3-5

3) Not only so, but we also rejoice in our sufferings, *because we know that suffering produces perseverance;*
4) *perseverance, character; and character, hope.*
5) And hope does not disappoint us, because God has poured out his love into our hearts by the Holy Spirit, whom he has given us.

Jam 1:12

12) Blessed is the man who perseveres under trial, because *when he has stood the test, he will receive the crown of life that God has promised to those who love him.*

1Ths 3:2-4

2) We sent Timothy, who is our brother and God's fellow worker in spreading the gospel of Christ, *to strengthen and encourage you in your faith,*

3) *so that no one would be unsettled by these trials. You know quite well that we were destined for them.*

4) In fact, when we were with you, we kept telling you that we would be persecuted. And it turned out that way, as you well know.

2Tim 3:12-13

12) *In fact, everyone who wants to live a godly life in Christ Jesus will be persecuted,*

13) while evil men and impostors will go from bad to worse, deceiving and being deceived.

Jam 5:10-11

10) Brothers, as an example of patience in the face of suffering, take the prophets who spoke in the name of the Lord.

11) *As you know, we consider blessed those who have persevered. You have heard of Job's perseverance and have seen what the Lord finally brought about. The Lord is full of compassion and mercy.*

2Cor 1:8-10

8) We do not want you to be uninformed, brothers, about the hardships we suffered in the province of Asia. We were under great pressure, far beyond our ability to endure, so that we despaired even of life.

9) Indeed, in our hearts we felt the sentence of death. *But this happened that we might not rely on ourselves but on God,* who raises the dead.

10) He has delivered us from such a deadly peril, and he will deliver us. On him we have set our hope that he will continue to deliver us,

2Cor 4:16-18

16) Therefore we do not lose heart. Though outwardly we are wasting away, yet inwardly we are being renewed day by day.

17) *For our light and momentary troubles are achieving for us an eternal glory that far outweighs them all.*

18) So we fix our eyes not on what is seen, but on what is unseen. For what is seen is temporary, but what is unseen is eternal.

1Pet 1:6-7

6) In this you greatly rejoice, though now for a little while you may have had to suffer grief in all kinds of trials.

7) *These have come so that your faith—of greater worth than gold, which perishes even though refined by fire—may be proved genuine and may result in praise, glory and honor when Jesus Christ is revealed.*

2Cor 1:3-5

3) Praise be to the God and Father of our Lord Jesus Christ, the Father of compassion and the God of all comfort,

4) *who comforts us in all our troubles, so that we can comfort those in any trouble with the comfort we ourselves have received from God.*

5) For just as the sufferings of Christ flow over into our lives, so also through Christ our comfort overflows.

2Cor 4:7-9

7) But we have this treasure in jars of clay *to show that this all-surpassing power is from God and not from us.*

8) We are hard pressed on every side, but not crushed; perplexed, but not in despair;

9) persecuted, but not abandoned; struck down, but not destroyed.

Heb 12:1-4

1) Therefore, since we are surrounded by such a great cloud of witnesses, let us throw off everything that hinders and the sin that so easily entangles, *and let us run with perseverance the race marked out for us.*

2) Let us fix our eyes on Jesus, the author and perfecter of our faith, *who for the joy set before him endured the cross,* scorning its shame, and sat down at the right hand of the throne of God.

3) *Consider him who endured such opposition from sinful men, so that you will not grow weary and lose heart.*

4) In your struggle against sin, you have not yet resisted to the point of shedding your blood.

Heb 4:15-16

15) For we do not have a high priest who is unable to sympathize with our weaknesses, *but we have one who has been tempted in every way, just as we are—yet was without sin.*

16) Let us then approach the throne of grace with confidence, so that we may receive mercy and find grace to help us in our time of need.

Job 14:1

1) "Man born of woman is of few days and full of trouble."

Jam 4:10

10) Humble yourselves before the Lord, and he will lift
   you up.

*Note: *italics* added to relate to topic title; author
comments in parentheses to clarify

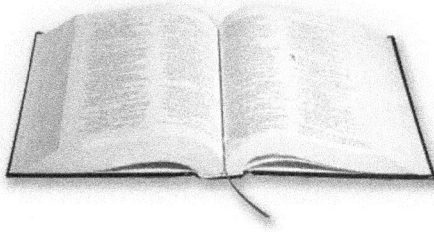

God is omnipresent and all-knowing

Psa 33:13-15

13) From heaven the LORD looks down and sees all mankind;

14) from his dwelling place he watches all who live on earth—

15) *he who forms the hearts of all, who considers everything they do.*

Psa 139:1-12

1) O LORD, you have searched me and you know me.

2) You know when I sit and when I rise; you perceive my thoughts from afar.

3) You discern my going out and my lying down; *you are familiar with all my ways.*

4) Before a word is on my tongue you know it completely, O LORD.

5) You hem me in—behind and before; you have laid your hand upon me.

6) *Such knowledge is too wonderful for me, too lofty for me to attain.*

7) *Where can I go from your Spirit? Where can I flee from your presence?*

8) If I go up to the heavens, you are there; if I make my bed in the depths, you are there.

9) If I rise on the wings of the dawn, if I settle on the far side of the sea,
10) even there your hand will guide me, your right hand will hold me fast.

11) If I say, "Surely the darkness will hide me and the light become night around me,"
12) *even the darkness will not be dark to you; the night will shine like the day, for darkness is as light to you.*

Isa 29:15-16

15) Woe to those who go to great depths to hide their plans from the LORD, who do their work in darkness and think, *"Who sees us? Who will know?"*
16) You turn things upside down, as if the potter were thought to be like the clay! Shall what is formed say to him who formed it, "He did not make me"? Can the pot say of the potter, "He knows nothing"?

Jer 23:23-24

23) "Am I only a God nearby," declares the LORD, "and not a God far away?
24) Can anyone hide in secret places so that I cannot see him?" declares the LORD. *"Do not I fill heaven and earth?" declares the LORD.*

2Chr 16:9

9) For the eyes of the LORD range throughout the earth *to strengthen those whose hearts are fully committed to him.....*

Job 34:21

21) "His eyes are on the ways of men; he sees their every step.

Prov 5:21

21) For a man's ways are in full view of the LORD, and he examines all his paths.

Prov 15:3

3) The eyes of the LORD are everywhere, keeping watch on the wicked and the good.

Prov 16:2

2) All a man's ways seem innocent to him, *but motives are weighed by the LORD.*

Prov 24:12

12) If you say, "But we knew nothing about this," does not he who weighs the heart perceive it? Does not he who guards your life know it? Will he not repay each person according to what he has done?

Jer 17:10

10) *"I the LORD search the heart and examine the mind,* to reward a man according to his conduct, according to what his deeds deserve."

Psa 94:9-10

9) Does he who implanted the ear not hear? Does he who formed the eye not see?

10) Does he who disciplines nations not punish? *Does he who teaches man lack knowledge?*

Luke 12:2-3

2) *There is nothing concealed that will not be disclosed, or hidden that will not be made known.*

3) What you have said in the dark will be heard in the daylight, and what you have whispered in the ear in the inner rooms will be proclaimed from the roofs.

1Cor 4:4-5

4) My conscience is clear, but that does not make me innocent. It is the Lord who judges me.

5) Therefore judge nothing before the appointed time; wait till the Lord comes. *He will bring to light what is hidden in darkness and will expose the motives of men's hearts.* At that time each will receive his praise from God.

Amos 4:13

13) He who forms the mountains, creates the wind, and reveals his thoughts to man, he who turns dawn to darkness, and treads the high places of the earth— *the LORD God Almighty is his name.*

(in our daily lives we sometimes encounter an unusually big and muscular man, and often think to ourselves, "oh my, you don't want to mess with him". By the same token, give some thought to the size, knowledge, and power of our one and only God as shown in the verses above...it is absolutely eye-opening and difficult to comprehend. He is the ultimate Chairman-of-the-Board.

And yet, every day, millions/billions of us ignore God completely, or follow his principles only until they infringe on current pleasures, or glibly flip him off as irrelevant to modern times where "do-your-own-thing" is the mantra being heard 'round the world.

But wait just a moment, consider this...anybody who *seriously reads the verses above in this topic* should plainly see that all people who glibly "mess with almighty God" have some very real surprises in store for themselves when judgment day arrives. If we think *a man* can be big and muscular, just wait until we meet God himself in person)

1Pet 5:6

6) Humble yourselves, therefore, *under God's mighty hand*, that he may lift you up in due time.

("humble" = the opposite of self-pride and egotism; unpretentious)

*Note: *italics* added to relate to topic title; author comments in parentheses to clarify

God's discipline and reproof

Deut 8:2-5

2) Remember how the LORD your God led you all the way in the desert these forty years, *to humble you and to test you in order to know what was in your heart,* whether or not you would keep his commands.

3) He humbled you, causing you to hunger and then feeding you with manna, which neither you nor your fathers had known, *to teach you that man does not live on bread alone but on every word that comes from the mouth of the LORD.*

4) Your clothes did not wear out and your feet did not swell during these forty years.

5) *Know then in your heart that as a man disciplines his son, so the LORD your God disciplines you.*

Prov 15:32

32) He who ignores discipline despises himself, *but whoever heeds correction gains understanding.*

Prov 3:11-12

11) *My son, do not despise the LORD's discipline and do not resent his rebuke,*

12) *because the LORD disciplines those he loves, as a father the son he delights in.*

Eccl 11:9

9) Be happy, young man, while you are young, and let your heart give you joy in the days of your youth. Follow the ways of your heart and whatever your eyes see, *but know that for all these things God will bring you to judgment.*

Psa 25:8

8) Good and upright is the LORD; *therefore he instructs sinners in his ways.*

Lam 3:31-33

31) For men are not cast off by the Lord forever.
32) Though he brings grief, he will show compassion, so great is his unfailing love.
33) For he does not willingly bring affliction or grief to the children of men.

Psa 30:5

5) For his anger lasts only a moment, but his favor lasts a lifetime; *weeping may remain for a night, but rejoicing comes in the morning.*

Prov 27:17

17) As iron sharpens iron, so one man sharpens another.

(if someone upsets us or tries our patience to the breaking point, it is quite likely God caused the person to cross our path in order to increase in us that *same patience,* plus self-control and forgiveness of other people's unique faults...just as we also must be forgiven by God for our own shortcomings. It does not mean we must be "friendly" with them; just understanding of worldly human nature) see next entry.

Psa 139:23-24

23) Search me, O God, and know my heart; *test me and know my anxious thoughts.*

24) *See if there is any offensive way in me*, and lead me in the way everlasting.

Luke 8:20-21

20) Someone told him, "Your mother and brothers are standing outside, wanting to see you."

21) He replied, *"My mother and brothers are those who hear God's word and put it into practice."*

(this reproof shows the ironclad single-mindedness Jesus had for his Father in heaven. When the choice comes down to pleasing people versus pleasing God, the answer is clear.

The most important decisions we face in this life are: accepting God's forgiveness through Christ for our wrong-doings, or not; then following his teachings in the Bible, or not. Decisions which are even more important than our relatives, who must make the same ones themselves)

Luke 9:59-62

59) He said to another man, "Follow me." But the man replied, "Lord, first let me go and bury my father."

60) Jesus said to him, "Let the dead bury their own dead, but you go and proclaim the kingdom of God."

61) Still another said, "I will follow you, Lord; but first let me go back and say good-by to my family."

62) Jesus replied, "No one who puts his hand to the plow and looks back is fit for service in the kingdom of God."

(see comment above, as these verses speak to the same disciplinary principle)

1Cor 11:32

32) When we are judged by the Lord, *we are being disciplined so that we will not be condemned with the world.*

Rev 3:19

19) Those whom I love I rebuke and discipline. *So be earnest, and repent.*

2Cor 7:8-10

8) Even if I caused you sorrow by my letter, I do not regret it. Though I did regret it—I see that my letter hurt you, but only for a little while—

9) yet now I am happy, not because you were made sorry, but because your sorrow led you to repentance. For you became sorrowful as God intended and so were not harmed in any way by us.

10) *Godly sorrow brings repentance that leads to salvation and leaves no regret, but worldly sorrow brings death.*

Heb 12:4-8

4) In your struggle against sin, you have not yet resisted to the point of shedding your blood.

5) *And you have forgotten that word of encouragement that addresses you as sons: "My son, do not make light of the Lord's discipline, and do not lose heart when he rebukes you,*

6) *because the Lord disciplines those he loves, and he punishes everyone he accepts as a son."*

7) Endure hardship as discipline; God is treating you as sons. For what son is not disciplined by his father?

8) *If you are not disciplined (and everyone undergoes discipline), then you are illegitimate children and not true sons.*

Heb 12:11

11) No discipline seems pleasant at the time, but painful. *Later on, however, it produces a harvest of righteousness and peace for those who have been trained by it.*

1Tim 3:1-7

1) Here is a trustworthy saying: If anyone sets his heart on being an overseer, he desires a noble task.

2) Now the overseer must be above reproach, the husband of but one wife, temperate, self-controlled, respectable, hospitable, able to teach,

3) not given to drunkenness, not violent but gentle, not quarrelsome, not a lover of money.

4) He must manage his own family well and see that his children obey him with proper respect.

5) (If anyone does not know how to manage his own family, how can he take care of God's church?)

6) He must not be a recent convert, or he may become conceited and fall under the same judgment as the devil.

7) He must also have a good reputation with outsiders, so that he will not fall into disgrace and into the devil's trap.

(these verses are an excellent definition of Christian character and self-discipline)

*Note: *italics* added to relate to topic title; author comments in parentheses to clarify

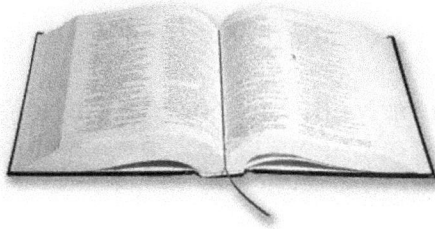

Hell - reality and agony

(This topic is difficult for most of us to deal with, and yet one the Word of God plainly states is indeed a reality. We have been given a *free will* to choose either to face that reality now before we die, or as revealed below, wait until we stand before God on Judgment day, which of course will be too late to change our destiny.

It needs to be clearly understood that <u>we</u> make the choice, not God. He has provided the way to escape from eternal death... Jesus Christ's sacrifice on our behalf is a *free gift*, and available to everyone worldwide, but God does not force us to take it)

Mat 7:13-14
13) "Enter through the narrow gate. For wide is the gate and broad is the road that leads to destruction, and many enter through it.
14) But small is the gate and narrow the road that leads to life, and only a few find it.

Mat 10:28
28) Do not be afraid of those who kill the body but cannot kill the soul. *Rather, be afraid of the One who can destroy both soul and body in hell.*

Mat 13:40-43

40) "As the weeds are pulled up and burned in the fire, so it will be at the end of the age.

41) The Son of Man will send out his angels, and they will weed out of his kingdom everything that causes sin and all who do evil.

42) They will throw them into the fiery furnace, *where there will be weeping and gnashing of teeth.*

43) Then the righteous will shine like the sun in the kingdom of their Father. *He who has ears, let him hear.*

Mat 18:8-9

8) If your hand or your foot causes you to sin, cut it off and throw it away. *It is better for you to enter life maimed or crippled than to have two hands or two feet and be thrown into eternal fire.*

9) And if your eye causes you to sin, gouge it out and throw it away. *It is better for you to enter life with one eye than to have two eyes and be thrown into the fire of hell.*

2Ths 1:8-9

8) He will punish those who do not know God and do not obey the gospel of our Lord Jesus.

9) *They will be punished with everlasting destruction and shut out from the presence of the Lord and from the majesty of his power*

2Pet 2:4-9

4) For if God did not spare angels when they sinned, but sent them to hell, putting them into gloomy dungeons to be held for judgment;

5) if he did not spare the ancient world when he brought the flood on its ungodly people, but protected Noah, a preacher of righteousness, and seven others;

6) if he condemned the cities of Sodom and Gomorrah by burning them to ashes, and made them an example of what is going to happen to the ungodly;

7) and if he rescued Lot, a righteous man, who was distressed by the filthy lives of lawless men

8) (for that righteous man, living among them day after day, was tormented in his righteous soul by the lawless deeds he saw and heard)—

9) *if this is so, then the Lord knows how to rescue godly men from trials and to hold* the unrighteous for the day of judgment, while continuing their punishment.

Luke 16:19-26

19) "There was a rich man who was dressed in purple and fine linen and lived in luxury every day.

20) At his gate was laid a beggar named Lazarus, covered with sores

21) and longing to eat what fell from the rich man's table. Even the dogs came and licked his sores.

22) "The time came when the beggar died and the angels carried him to Abraham's side. The rich man also died and was buried.

23) In hell, where he was in torment, he looked up and saw Abraham far away, with Lazarus by his side.

24) *So he called to him, 'Father Abraham, have pity on me and send Lazarus to dip the tip of his finger in water and cool my tongue, because I am in agony in this fire.'*

25) "But Abraham replied, 'Son, remember that in your lifetime you received your good things, while Lazarus received bad things, but now he is comforted here and you are in agony.

26) *And besides all this, between us and you a great chasm has been fixed, so that those who want to go from here to you cannot, nor can anyone cross over from there to us.'*

(being rich is not what caused this man to land in hell; rather it was because he apparently showed no compassion or mercy to help the beggar. Rich or poor, it is the attitude of our hearts that matters to God) see entry below.

Mat 25:40-43

40) "The King will reply, 'I tell you the truth, whatever you did for one of the least of these brothers of mine, you did for me.'

41) *"Then he will say to those on his left, 'Depart from me, you who are cursed, into the eternal fire prepared for the devil and his angels.*

42) For I was hungry and you gave me nothing to eat, I was thirsty and you gave me nothing to drink,

43) I was a stranger and you did not invite me in, I needed clothes and you did not clothe me, I was sick and in prison and you did not look after me.'

Isa 33:14-16

14) The sinners in Zion are terrified; trembling grips the godless: *"Who of us can dwell with the consuming fire? Who of us can dwell with everlasting burning?"*

15) He who walks righteously and speaks what is right, who rejects gain from extortion and keeps his hand from accepting bribes, who stops his ears against plots of murder and shuts his eyes against contemplating evil—

16) *this is the man who will dwell on the heights, whose refuge will be the mountain fortress. His bread will be supplied, and water will not fail him.*

Rev 20:12-15

12) And I saw the dead, great and small, standing before the throne, and books were opened. Another book was opened, which is the book of life. *The dead were judged according to what they had done as recorded in the books.*

13) The sea gave up the dead that were in it, and death and Hades gave up the dead that were in them, and each person was judged according to what he had done.

14) Then death and Hades were thrown into the lake of fire. The lake of fire is the second death.

15) *If anyone's name was not found written in the book of life, he was thrown into the lake of fire.*

(over the course of a lifetime all people are guilty of many wrongdoings *in God's eyes*, which results in human beings, including our leaders, being a "fallen" race in a world dominated by our various self-centered interests and mistaken choices.

This leads to unending "people-problems" everywhere... trouble at home or at work or with the neighbors, divorce, sickness, materialism and greed, ego/pride, hyper-sexuality, judging others, impatience, envy, anger, poverty, crime, terrorism, and on and on to name just some of Mankind's self-induced problems. The final outcome of all this distortion from "normal", as humans were originally created, is death and separation from God forever by not being named in the Book of Life.

Separated, that is, until we accept God's gift of Jesus Christ who, <u>as our substitute</u>, took the punishment God states we each deserve. *But when we believe in Christ's sacrifice on the cross as being in our place, and in his resurrection from the dead to another life, we are then 100% pardoned from our wrongdoings and for ignoring God in our daily lives.*

Once we receive this unearned blessing, God *does expect* Believers to put forth effort to learn more about his Word in the Bible, and the kinds of attitudes, habits, and lifestyles that not only please him, but are for our own good as well. But that is a gradual, lifelong process we experience day-by-day as God's inner Spirit molds us into kinder, gentler people—which we come to cherish.

It obviously behooves each of us to accept this free gift of everlasting life, offered by a loving God reaching out to redeem his wayward creation. When we realize how valuable the offer is it should be an easy, logical decision.

Remember this: the skeletons of all other religious founders or leaders or preachers are still in their graves, awaiting the end-time opening of the Book of Life, just like the rest of us will be. Only Jesus Christ was resurrected to show us another life)

*Note: *italics* added to relate to topic title; author comments in parentheses to clarify

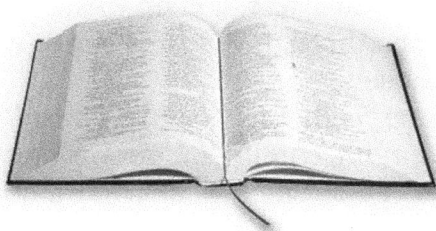

Resurrection of dead -
eternal life

2Sam 14:14

14) Like water spilled on the ground, which cannot be recovered, so we must die. But God does not take away life; *instead, he devises ways so that a banished person may not remain estranged from him.*

Mal 3:16-18

16) Then those who feared the LORD talked with each other, and the LORD listened and heard. A scroll of remembrance was written in his presence concerning those who feared the LORD and honored his name.

17) *"They will be mine," says the LORD Almighty, "in the day when I make up my treasured possession. I will spare them, just as in compassion a man spares his son who serves him.*

18) And you will again see the distinction between the righteous and the wicked, between those who serve God and those who do not.

(for anyone looking for a reason to "respect and honor the Lord", the above verses qualify)

Act 1:1-3

1) In my former book, Theophilus, I wrote about all that Jesus began to do and to teach

2) until the day he was taken up to heaven, after giving instructions through the Holy Spirit to the apostles he had chosen.

3) *After his suffering, he showed himself to these men and gave many convincing proofs that he was alive. He appeared to them over a period of forty days and spoke about the kingdom of God.*

(Luke, writing about the 12 apostles who would be Christ's eyewitnesses to the nations, after seeing his resurrected body many times in person)

John 5:24

24) "I tell you the truth, whoever hears my word and believes him who sent me has eternal life and will not be condemned; *he has crossed over from death to life.*

John 6:39-40

39) And this is the will of him who sent me, that I shall lose none of all that he has given me, but raise them up at the last day.

40) For my Father's will is that *everyone who looks to the Son and believes in him shall have eternal life, and I will raise him up at the last day.*"

John 11:25-27

25) Jesus said to her, "I am the resurrection and the life. *He who believes in me will live, even though he dies;*

26) *and whoever lives and believes in me will never die.* Do you believe this?"

27) "Yes, Lord," she told him, "I believe that you are the Christ, the Son of God, who was to come into the world."

John 14:1-3

1) "Do not let your hearts be troubled. Trust in God; trust also in me.

2) In my Father's house are many rooms; if it were not so, I would have told you. *I am going there to prepare a place for you.*

3) *And if I go and prepare a place for you, I will come back and take you to be with me that you also may be where I am.*

Act 2:22-24

22) "Men of Israel, listen to this: Jesus of Nazareth was a man accredited by God to you by miracles, wonders and signs, which God did among you through him, as you yourselves know.

23) *This man was handed over to you by God's set purpose and foreknowledge*; and you, with the help of wicked men, put him to death by nailing him to the cross.

24) *But God raised him from the dead, freeing him from the agony of death, because it was impossible for death to keep its hold on him.*

Rom 8:10-11

10) *But if Christ is in you, your body is dead because of sin, yet your spirit is alive* because of righteousness.

11) And if the Spirit of him who raised Jesus from the dead is living in you, *he who raised Christ from the dead will also give life to your mortal bodies through his Spirit, who lives in you.*

1Cor 15:42-44

42) So will it be with the resurrection of the dead. The body that is sown is perishable, it is raised imperishable;

43) it is sown in dishonor, it is raised in glory; it is sown in weakness, it is raised in power;

44) it is sown a natural body, it is raised a spiritual body. *If there is a natural body, there is also a spiritual body.*

1Cor 15:51-53

51) Listen, I tell you a mystery: We will not all sleep, but we will all be changed—

52) in a flash, in the twinkling of an eye, at the last trumpet. *For the trumpet will sound, the dead will be raised imperishable, and we will be changed.*

53) For the perishable must clothe itself with the imperishable, and the mortal with immortality.

Php 3:20-21

20) But our citizenship is in heaven. And we eagerly await a Savior from there, the Lord Jesus Christ,

21) who, by the power that enables him to bring everything under his control, *will transform our lowly bodies so that they will be like his glorious body.*

1Ths 4:13-18

13) Brothers, we do not want you to be ignorant about those who fall asleep, or to grieve like the rest of men, who have no hope.

14) We believe that Jesus died and rose again and so we believe that God will bring with Jesus those who have fallen asleep in him.

15) According to the Lord's own word, we tell you that we who are still alive, who are left till the coming of the Lord, will certainly not precede those who have fallen asleep.

16) For the Lord himself will come down from heaven, with a loud command, with the voice of the archangel and with the trumpet call of God, and the dead in Christ will rise first.

17) After that, we who are still alive and are left will be caught up together with them in the clouds to meet the Lord in the air. And so we will be with the Lord forever.

18) Therefore encourage each other with these words.

Heb 9:27-28

27) Just as man is destined to die once, and after that to face judgment,

28) so Christ was sacrificed once to take away the sins of many people; and he will appear a second time, not to bear sin, *but to bring salvation to those who are waiting for him.*

Dan 12:2

2) Multitudes who sleep in the dust of the earth will awake: *some to everlasting life, others to shame and everlasting contempt.*

Rev 5:9-10

9) And they sang a new song: "You are worthy to take the scroll and to open its seals, because you were slain, and with your blood you purchased men for God from every tribe and language and people and nation.

10) *You have made them to be a kingdom and priests to serve our God, and they will reign on the earth.*"

*Note: *italics* added to relate to topic title; author comments in parentheses to clarify

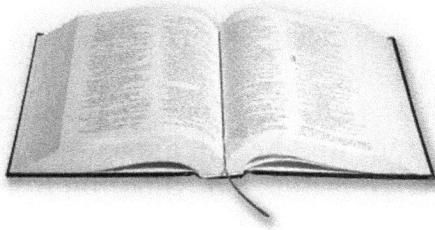

End of the age - new earth

Mat 24:3-15

3) As Jesus was sitting on the Mount of Olives, the disciples came to him privately. "Tell us," they said, "when will this happen, and what will be the sign of your coming and of the end of the age?"

4) Jesus answered: "Watch out that no one deceives you.

5) For many will come in my name, claiming, 'I am the Christ,' and will deceive many.

6) You will hear of wars and rumors of wars, but see to it that you are not alarmed. *Such things must happen, but the end is still to come.*

7) Nation will rise against nation, and kingdom against kingdom. There will be famines and earthquakes in various places.

8) *All these are the beginning of birth pains.*

9) *"Then you will be handed over to be persecuted and put to death, and you will be hated by all nations because of me.*

10) *At that time many will turn away from the faith and will betray and hate each other,*

11) and many false prophets will appear and deceive many people.

12) *Because of the increase of wickedness, the love of most will grow cold,*
13) but he who stands firm to the end will be saved.
14) And this gospel of the kingdom will be preached in the whole world as a testimony to all nations, *and then the end will come.*
15) *"So when you see standing in the holy place 'the abomination that causes desolation,'* spoken of through the prophet Daniel—let the reader understand— .....

Mat 24:21-33

21) *For then there will be great distress, unequaled from the beginning of the world until now—and never to be equaled again.*
22) If those days had not been cut short, no one would survive, *but for the sake of the elect those days will be shortened.*
23) At that time if anyone says to you, 'Look, here is the Christ!' or, 'There he is!' do not believe it.
24) For false Christs and false prophets will appear and perform great signs and miracles to deceive even the elect—if that were possible.
25) See, I have told you ahead of time.
26) "So if anyone tells you, 'There he is, out in the desert,' do not go out; or, 'Here he is, in the inner rooms,' do not believe it.
27) For as lightning that comes from the east is visible even in the west, so will be the coming of the Son of Man.
28) Wherever there is a carcass, there the vultures will gather.

29) *"Immediately after the distress of those days "'the sun will be darkened, and the moon will not give its light; the stars will fall from the sky, and the heavenly bodies will be shaken.'*

30) *"At that time the sign of the Son of Man will appear in the sky*, and all the nations of the earth will mourn. They will see the Son of Man coming on the clouds of the sky, with power and great glory.

31) And he will send his angels with a loud trumpet call, and *they will gather his elect* from the four winds, from one end of the heavens to the other.

32) "Now learn this lesson from the fig tree: As soon as its twigs get tender and its leaves come out, you know that summer is near.

33) *Even so, when you see all these things, you know that it is near, right at the door.*

(see entries below for more explanation on the above verses)

2Ths 2:1-4

1) Concerning the coming of our Lord Jesus Christ and our being gathered to him, we ask you, brothers,

2) not to become easily unsettled or alarmed by some prophecy, report or letter supposed to have come from us, saying that the day of the Lord has already come.

3) Don't let anyone deceive you in any way, for *that day will not come until the* rebellion occurs and the man of lawlessness is revealed, the man doomed to destruction.

4) He will oppose and will exalt himself over everything that is called God or is worshiped, so that he sets himself up in God's temple, proclaiming himself to be God.

(the "man of lawlessness" above *who will claim to be God* is the same as the "lawless one" in the next entry below, commonly known as the "anti-Christ".

"That day will not come until the rebellion occurs" relates to extreme persecution of Christian Believers, led by the anti-Christ, causing many to "turn away from the faith and betray each other", as stated above in Mat 24: 9-15. This will occur during the time of "great distress", also known as the "tribulation" period, referred to above in Mat 24:21-33, which ends with shocking signs in heaven, the sun, moon, and stars, plus the second coming of Christ to earth...see vs 29-30.

This entire end-time period, with its many horrible plagues sent from God onto non-believers, is graphically detailed with symbolic language found in Rev: chapters 4-19).

2Ths 2:9-12

9) *The coming of the lawless one will be in accordance with the work of Satan displayed in all kinds of counterfeit miracles, signs and wonders,*

10) *and in every sort of evil that deceives those who are perishing. They perish because they refused to love the truth and so be saved.*

11) For this reason God sends them a powerful delusion so that they will believe the lie

12) and so that all will be condemned who have not believed the truth but have delighted in wickedness.

(an end finally comes to the period of "great distress". But there is still one last phase to play out for planet earth in its present form...*the thousand-year reign of Christ on earth after his return.*

He will be joined by those people who are slain for remaining true to him during the "great distress" period, stated below in **Rev 20:4**, plus any survivors as noted in Mat 24:9-13 & 22 above—their reward, no doubt, for being faithful.

Then after the thousand-year reign and the final destruction of Satan, we will all be raised to stand before the great white throne judgment of God the Father, and receive our own rewards, depending on whether we have acted on the truth of Jesus Christ, or not.

Entry below describes this final period before heaven and
earth are re-created)

Rev 20:1-15

1) And I saw an angel coming down out of heaven,
having the key to the Abyss and holding in his hand
a great chain.

2) *He seized the dragon, that ancient serpent, who is
the devil, or Satan, and bound him for a thousand
years.*

3) He threw him into the Abyss, and locked and sealed
it over him, to keep him from deceiving the nations
anymore until the thousand years were ended. *After
that, he must be set free for a short time.*

4) I saw thrones on which were seated those who had
been given authority to judge. And I saw the souls
of those who had been beheaded because of their
testimony for Jesus and because of the word of God.
They had not worshiped the beast or his image and
had not received his mark on their foreheads or their
hands. *They came to life and reigned with Christ a
thousand years.*

5) *(The rest of the dead did not come to life until
the thousand years were ended.)* This is the first
resurrection.

6) Blessed and holy are those who have part in the first
resurrection. The second death has no power over
them, but they will be priests of God and of Christ
and *will reign with him for a thousand years.*

7) *When the thousand years are over, Satan will be
released from his prison*

8) and will go out to deceive the nations in the four
corners of the earth—Gog and Magog—to gather
them for battle. In number they are like the sand on
the seashore.

9) They marched across the breadth of the earth and surrounded the camp of God's people, the city he loves. *But fire came down from heaven and devoured them.*

10) And the devil, who deceived them, was thrown into the lake of burning sulfur, where the beast and the false prophet had been thrown. *They will be tormented day and night for ever and ever.*

11) Then I saw a great white throne and him who was seated on it. Earth and sky fled from his presence, and there was no place for them.

12) *And I saw the dead, great and small, standing before the throne, and books were opened. Another book was opened, which is the book of life. The dead were judged according to what they had done as recorded in the books.*

13) The sea gave up the dead that were in it, and death and Hades gave up the dead that were in them, and each person was judged according to what he had done.

14) Then death and Hades were thrown into the lake of fire. The lake of fire is the second death.

15) *If anyone's name was not found written in the book of life, he was thrown into the lake of fire.*

Rev 21:1-5

1) *Then I saw a new heaven and a new earth,* for the first heaven and the first earth had passed away, and there was no longer any sea.

2) I saw the Holy City, the new Jerusalem, coming down out of heaven from God, prepared as a bride beautifully dressed for her husband.

3) And I heard a loud voice from the throne saying, *"Now the dwelling of God is with* men, and he will live with them. They will be his people, and God himself will be with them and be their God.

4) He will wipe every tear from their eyes. There will be no more death or mourning or crying or pain, for the old order of things has passed away."

5) He who was seated on the throne said, "I am making everything new!" Then he said, "Write this down, for these words are trustworthy and true."

(these verses clearly show all Believers there is a future life awaiting us that will make all previous suffering, whatever its form, worth enduring in the end. *"No more death or mourning or crying or pain"* are wonderful reasons to keep the faith until our final rest.

*The following entries show what to expect from ungodly people in the years leading up to and including the final end-of-the-age period explained above in this topic)

2Tim 3:1-5

1) But mark this: There will be terrible times in the last days.

2) People will be lovers of themselves, lovers of money, boastful, proud, abusive, disobedient to their parents, ungrateful, unholy,

3) without love, unforgiving, slanderous, without self-control, brutal, not lovers of the good,

4) treacherous, rash, conceited, lovers of pleasure rather than lovers of God—

5) having a form of godliness but denying its power. *Have nothing to do with them.*

(a brutal description of what the "cancer of sin" will do after it has spread over the earth for thousands of years, making people more like wild animals than human beings. The question of the day is how much of this demand-my-own-way spirit are we seeing today in current society? How much more to come before God steps in? It's not only worth thinking about, it's worth much self-examination as well) see below.

Luke 17:26-30

26) "Just as it was in the days of Noah, so also will it be in the days of the Son of Man.

27) *People were eating, drinking, marrying and being given in marriage up to the day Noah entered the ark. Then the flood came and destroyed them all.*

28) "It was the same in the days of Lot. *People were eating and drinking, buying and selling, planting and building.*

29) But the day Lot left Sodom, fire and sulfur rained down from heaven and destroyed them all.

30) *"It will be just like this on the day the Son of Man is revealed.*

(the usual daily cares and self-pleasures; *not a moment's thought acknowledging God's presence in their lives*)

2Pet 3:10

10) But the day of the Lord will come like a thief. The heavens will disappear with a roar; the elements will be destroyed by fire, and the earth and everything in it will be laid bare.

*Note: *italics* added to relate to topic title; author comments in parentheses to clarify

God is Sovereign Ruler

Psa 90:2

2) Before the mountains were born or you brought forth the earth and the world, *from everlasting to everlasting you are God.*

Neh 9:6

6) You alone are the LORD. You made the heavens, even the highest heavens, and all their starry host, the earth and all that is on it, the seas and all that is in them. *You give life to everything, and the multitudes of heaven worship you.*

Eph 3:8-10

8) Although I am less than the least of all God's people, this grace was given me: to preach to the Gentiles the unsearchable riches of Christ,

9) and to make plain to everyone the administration of this mystery, which for ages past was kept hidden in God, who created all things.

10) *His intent was that now, through the church, the manifold wisdom of God should be made known to the rulers and authorities in the heavenly realms,*

(made known to those *in heaven* remaining loyal to God, who withstood Satan's rebellion and expulsion to earth, and have gotten to watch daily the destructive results of *having someone other than God be in charge*...namely

Mankind, as this mostly self-centered and power-driven "stage play" on planet earth has unfolded to the *heavenly rulers and authorities* one year at a time.

However, all the wrongdoings of the human race through-out history have only served to showcase God's compassion and grace all the more. He has always provided a way of escape; a way for each person to receive forgiveness, if only we will choose to receive it and live it) see Rom 5: 8-10.

Psa 115:16

16) The highest heavens belong to the LORD, *but the earth he has given to man.* (see entry above)

Act 17:24-27

24) "The God who made the world and everything in it is the Lord of heaven and earth and does not live in temples built by hands.

25) And he is not served by human hands, as if he needed anything, because he himself gives all men life and breath and everything else.

26) From one man he made every nation of men, that they should inhabit the whole earth; and he determined the times set for them and the exact places where they should live.

27) God did this so that men would seek him and perhaps reach out for him and find him, though he is not far from each one of us.

Job 11:7-8

7) "Can you fathom the mysteries of God? Can you probe the limits of the Almighty?

8) They are higher than the heavens—what can you do? They are deeper than the depths of the grave—what can you know?

Isa 55:8-9

8) "For my thoughts are not your thoughts, neither are your ways my ways," declares the LORD.

9) *"As the heavens are higher than the earth, so are my ways higher than your ways and my thoughts than your thoughts.*

Isa 40:12-15

12) Who has measured the waters in the hollow of his hand, or with the breadth of his hand marked off the heavens? Who has held the dust of the earth in a basket, or weighed the mountains on the scales and the hills in a balance?

13) Who has understood the mind of the LORD, or instructed him as his counselor?

14) Whom did the LORD consult to enlighten him, and who taught him the right way? Who was it that taught him knowledge or showed him the path of understanding?

15) *Surely the nations are like a drop in a bucket; they are regarded as dust on the scales; he weighs the islands as though they were fine dust.*

Isa 40:18

18) To whom, then, will you compare God? What image will you compare him to?

Rev 4:11

11) "You are worthy, our Lord and God, to receive glory and honor and power, *for you created all things, and by your will they were created and have their being."*

Eccl 3:14

14) I know that everything God does will endure forever; nothing can be added to it and nothing taken from it. *God does it so that men will revere him.*

Prov 16:4

4) The LORD works out everything for his own ends—even the wicked for a day of disaster.

Deut 32:4

4) He is the Rock, his works are perfect, and all his ways are just. A faithful God who does no wrong, upright and just is he.

Job 42:2-6

2) "I know that you can do all things; no plan of yours can be thwarted.

3) You asked, 'Who is this that obscures my counsel without knowledge?' *Surely I spoke of things I did not understand, things too wonderful for me to know.*

4) "You said, 'Listen now, and I will speak; I will question you, and you shall answer me.'

5) My ears had heard of you but now my eyes have seen you.

6) *Therefore I despise myself and repent in dust and ashes.*"

*Note: *italics* added to relate to topic title; author comments in parentheses to clarify

About the Researcher/Author

Wesley Pierce is one of millions of people who grew up with almost no knowledge of the Bible or the principles of God it contains. His parents were decent, law-abiding people like many others, but the Scriptures were never read at home, nor was church attendance a part of their lives. God and Jesus Christ were brought up only when used as curse-words; about the same at school as well.

After serving in the Navy, Wesley attended college and lived in California throughout his 20's until, at age 30, several circumstances came together which caused him to accept an acquaintance's suggestion to buy a Bible and read it for the first time. In so doing he became captivated by the human history it contained, by the common sense of God's principles, and by the mercy and obedience of Christ's sacrifice on the cross.

Shortly thereafter he moved back to the Midwest where his roots and his relatives were located. Since returning over 35 years ago, he has been a student of the Scriptures, plus a student of being led and blessed, or taught and disciplined by God's inner Spirit daily, as any seeker of God experiences. All the while he worked in the fields of marketing and manufacturing until his recent semi-retirement.

Wesley has one daughter, and refers to himself as simply an average citizen (adding that it puts him and many others in the same social class as the original 12 Disciples and early Believers). He plans to spend the rest of his earthly life encouraging people everywhere to... "know the truth, and the truth will set you free"...in the midst of a world full of human voices and opinions.